Samsung
GALAXY Note 3

The 100% Unofficial User Guide

By Aaron J. Halbert

GALAXY NOTE 3 is a trademark of Samsung Electronics Co., Ltd. All other trademarks and copyrights are the property of their respective owners.

Foreword

Thank you very much for purchasing *Samsung Galaxy Note 3: The 100% Unofficial User Guide*. I have worked hard to compile only the most relevant and useful information for you, and I firmly believe that you will get your money's worth. Better yet, when you are finished with this book, your skills and knowledge will put you among the top 1% of Note 3 power users.

If you have any feedback on this book, please feel absolutely free to email me at AJH@AaronHalbert.com or post a review on Amazon. By doing so, you will be helping all Note 3 users get the information they need, and you will also have my enduring gratitude. I carefully read and consider all the comments I get, because I believe in listening to my customers.

Before we begin, a couple things:

- Throughout this book, I sometimes suggest you purchase apps or accessories to improve your Note 3 experience. I am **NOT** affiliated with any of these companies, nor do I receive any sort of compensation from them. All of my recommendations are based on my own experience and research, and are completely independent.

- Please take a minute right now to sign up for my email mailing list. I will be sending out a Note 3 newsletter to all subscribers, containing the latest news, additional tips & tricks, and more! I will never sell or divulge your email address to any third parties.
  http://www.aaronhalbert.com/phplist/?p=subscribe&id=1

Table Of Contents

Chapter 1: Introduction

Thank you for purchasing *Samsung Galaxy Note 3: The 100% Unofficial User Guide!* This book is designed to help you unlock the potential of your Note 3 whether you're brand new to Android or a seasoned veteran.

TIP: Click any <u>underlined hyperlink</u> to jump to that section of the book.

Structure Of The Book

In Chapter 2, About The Note 3, this book situates the Note 3 in the Galaxy lineup, and in the history of mobile devices more generally. The Note 3 is a landmark device, and every user will benefit from understanding why.

Chapter 3, <u>Getting Started</u> (p.18), guides you through initial setup and helps you get your Note 3 up and running fast.

Chapter 4, <u>Fundamentals For New Users</u> (p. 33), is a crash course in TouchWiz and Android for first-time Android users.

Chapters 5-8, <u>Basic Functions</u> (p.65), <u>Intermediate Functions, Part 1</u> (p.182), <u>Intermediate Functions, Part 2</u> (p.216), and <u>Advanced Functions</u> (p.249), are the core of this book and cumulatively build your knowledge and skills with the Note 3.

Chapter 9, <u>What Are These Apps?</u> (p.283), provides brief reviews of the many apps that come with the Note 3. In some cases, I suggest alternatives.

In Chapter 10, <u>The 50 All-Time Best Android Apps</u>, (p.292) I recommend my 50 most-used third-party apps (i.e., apps that do not come pre-loaded on the Galaxy Note 3). All of these apps are very high quality and will appeal to many different types of users. This chapter includes the entirety of my book, *The 50 All-Time Best Android Apps*.

Finally, in Chapter 11, <u>Accessorizing</u> (p.308), I review the types of accessories available for the Note 3, highlight examples, and make some recommendations.

New Users Welcome!

With the Note 3, the truth is that novice and advanced users alike are on a pretty even playing field. As long as you understand the basics of Samsung's TouchWiz interface, which this book will thoroughly teach you, even beginners are not at a big disadvantage when it comes to the Note 3.

How can that possibly be?

The answer is that the Note 3 is unlike most Android devices. Samsung has packed the Note 3 with an incredible number of new capabilities, features, and apps that aren't found anywhere else except on a select few other new Samsung devices, such as the Galaxy S4. The options out-of-the-box border on overwhelming, and the breadth of possibilities can be unclear even for power users. To put it simply, there's just a ton of new stuff to learn, no matter how much experience you have.

TIP: TouchWiz refers to the software and themes that Samsung superimposes on the stock Android experience. If you want to compare TouchWiz with stock Android, compare your Note 3 to some screenshots of the Nexus 5. The differences aren't night and day—you can still recognize the Android OS—but nearly all of Google's stock apps have been replaced by customized Samsung equivalents, and the user interface has been tweaked to include S Pen and other features.

What Will You Get Out Of This?

Although it's possible to learn all of the features of the Note 3 through online research and experimentation, it's a lot faster and easier to use this book. I will tell you how each and every app and feature works, but I won't stop there. I will also tell you which are worthwhile and which are bloatware. I will suggest third-party alternatives that I trust.

If you are a brand new Android user and you don't know the Play Store from the App Drawer, this book will teach you from first principles. On the other hand, this book has everything you need if you're moving to the Note 3 from another device. Have you have ever asked yourself questions like:

- Is there ever a reason to use the Samsung App store instead of Google Play?

- Should I just use Google Now, or is S Voice actually worthwhile?

- Should I be using Samsung Kies? How do I even do so?

- What are the differences between NFC, S Beam, DLNA, and Wi-Fi Direct?

- What are AllShareCast and Group Play?

All of the answers are inside this book.

Who Am I?

Who am I, and what are my qualifications? First, I am a power user and enthusiast. I have owned and used nearly 10 different Android devices since Android first hit the market in 2008 on the T-Mobile G1. I have pushed each one to its limits, both in stock and rooted configurations, and I have taught countless others to do the same. In the decade before Android hit the market, I used numerous Windows Mobile and Palm OS phones and PDAs. In fact, I got my first one in 2002. I have written for several enthusiast websites, including one popular one that I started, owned, and ran in the early 2000s. This isn't my first rodeo; trust me when I say the Note 3 is one of the most complex devices to date.

Truly, I have never used another mobile device with so many programs and options available out of the box. Because of this, the possibilities have never been more exciting. The first smartphones were little more than glorified day planners; today, the Note 3 can do nearly any task that your home computer or laptop can do, *if you know how to use it*.

If you want to make the most of your Note 3, read this guide.

Chapter 2: About The Note 3

History And Philosophy

The Galaxy Note 3 is the third entry in Samsung's series of Note smartphones. From the start, the Note line has been distinguished from the more popular Galaxy S series by its large screen size and S Pen. (Samsung also manufactures a line of Android *tablets* under the name "Galaxy Note," including the Galaxy Note 10.1, Galaxy Note 8.0, and the recently released Galaxy Note 10.1 2014 Edition. These tablets share the S-Pen functionality of the Note smartphones, and run very similar software—they're just bigger and aren't phones.)

The concept of pen input is nothing new, but the Note series revived it after a period of dormancy. In the era of Palm OS devices, nearly every PDA and smartphone came with a stylus—a plastic pen that clipped into a slot on the device and was used to interact with the (monochrome or crude color LCD) touchscreen. These touchscreens used resistive technology; they sensed input by measuring pressure on the screen. Although it was possible to operate these touchscreens using your thumbnail, it was much easier to use a pointy object; hence, the stylus.

With the invention of the capacitive touchscreen—the type on all modern smartphones, which senses contact rather than pressure—it became possible to effectively use fingertips. The concept of pen input was abandoned, and even mocked. When Steve Jobs presented the first iPhone at Macworld 2007, he remarked, "Who wants a stylus? … [Yeechhhh!] Nobody wants a stylus [anymore]."

In many ways, Jobs was right. Styli can be clumsy and easy to lose. Capacitive touchscreens do improve the user experience in many ways. For example, they make thumb-based virtual keyboards possible. There is no doubt it is easier and faster to thumb-type than to peck on a virtual keyboard with a stylus, or to write one character at a time as with Graffiti in Palm OS.

At the same time, Jobs vastly oversimplified the issue. While capacitive touchscreens increase the convenience of the user experience, they also decrease the precision of input. The tip of your index finger is hundreds, if not thousands of times larger than the tip of a pencil. Jotting a quick note or sketching a diagram using a finger on a smartphone is clumsy and impractical. What Jobs forgot is that there is a reason human beings invented writing implements rather than dipping their fingers in ink.

In this way, stylus technology in mobile devices fell by the wayside—until Samsung revived it with the first Galaxy Note.

The first Galaxy Note smartphone, which debuted in early 2012 in the United States, introduced the two defining characteristics of the Galaxy Note line: a large screen and a stylus. In this way, Samsung combined the benefits of the finger-controlled capacitive touchscreen with the benefits of a precise input device. The first Galaxy Note featured a 5.3-inch screen and was available only on AT&T. It was the first "phablet" (portmanteau of "phone" and "tablet") to succeed commercially, selling more than 10 million units worldwide.

Samsung followed up with the Note 2 less than a year later, increasing the screen size to 5.5 inches and selling to customers on all major U.S. carriers. The Note 2 retained the core functionality of the first model—the phablet form factor and S Pen—but included significant hardware and performance upgrades, garnering very favorable reviews. It added interesting new functionality to the S Pen, such as Air View, permitting you to mimic mouse functionality by hovering over the screen with the S Pen. Even with the release of the Note 3, the Note 2 remains an impressive and capable device. As of the time of publication, Samsung has sold more than 30 million Note 2s, a threefold increase over the original model.

In October 2013, Samsung released the Note 3, the focus of this book.

Specifications

On the hardware side, Samsung increased the screen size from 5.5 to 5.7 inches by reducing the width of the bezel surrounding the screen, while maintaining nearly the same overall physical dimensions as the Note 2 and cutting the device's weight. The Note 3 received substantial performance upgrades, with a faster processor, a RAM increase from 2GB to 3GB, a higher resolution screen, boosted storage, and more. The table, below, shows the evolution of key specifications for the Galaxy Note line.

	Note 1	Note 2	Note 3
Size	146.9 x 83 x 9.7 mm	151.1 x 80.5 x 9.4 mm	151.2 x 79.2 x 8.3 mm
Weight	178g	182.5g	168g
Screen	5.3" HD Super AMOLED (1,280 x 800)	5.5" HD Super AMOLED (1,280 x 720)	5.7" Full HD Super AMOLED (1,920 x 1,080)
Storage	16 GB + microSD slot	16 / 32 / 64 GB + microSD slot	32 / 64 GB + microSD slot
Processor	1.4GHz Dual Core	1.6 GHz Quad-Core	2.3 GHz Quad-Core
RAM	1GB	2GB	3GB
Camera	8MP / 2MP Front	8MP / 1.9MP Front	13MP / 2MP Front
Battery	2,500 mAh	3,100 mAh	3,200 mAh

On the software side, the changes were more consequential for the user experience. First, the base OS has been upgraded from Jelly Bean 4.1 to Jelly Bean 4.3, adding security enhancements, Bluetooth 4.0 Low-Energy device support, OpenGL ES 3.0 support, and more. Second, Samsung included a truckload of new features in its TouchWiz interface, such as Pen Window, improved Multi Window, Action Memo, S Finder, Scrapbooker, glove mode, reading mode, and much, much more. Additionally, many features of the Note 2 have been modified or moved. For example, it was straightforward to use the equation recognition function of S Note on the Note 2, but this feature has been buried in Action Memo on the Note 3. This guide will explain every feature in detail, including how to find, configure, and use each one.

Distinguishing Features

In total, counting all of the various apps, settings, and capabilities available, it is fair to say that the Note 3 has hundreds of features. However, there is a core group of features around which Samsung is marketing the Note 3, and that differentiate it from the competition. And surprise—most of them relate to the S Pen. They include:

- **Air Command**: A new quick-access menu that you can activate with a click of the S Pen button, containing shortcuts to the most popular pen-based functions. In other words, Air Command is a portal for quickly calling up any of the functions of the S Pen. From the Air Command menu, you can launch Action Memo, Scrapbook, S Finder, Pen Window, or Screen Write, which are discussed below.

- **Action Memo**: Action Memo allows you to execute various commands based on information contained in handwritten memos, by leveraging the Note 3's handwriting recognition capabilities. For example, you can jot down a phone number and then instruct your phone to dial the number, add it to your contacts, e-mail it, or perform a number of other tasks using Action Memo.

- **Scrapbook**: The Scrapbook is a modern, electronic version of taking newspaper clippings. It allows you to save and consolidate text, images, and video from apps or websites into a centralized location on the device. This is accomplished by calling up the Scrapbooker button in Air Command and then circling the content you wish to save.

- **S Finder**: This is an app that lets you search the contents of the entire phone all at once. Without S Finder, you would have to open apps individually to search for information—for example, searching for "John" in the phone book would turn up John's contact information, but not any text messages or e-mails in which he participated. S Finder solves this problem by providing a centralized search function for all apps. Notably, S Finder even searches through handwritten content.

- **S Note**: S Note is the primary note-taking app on the Note 3. It differs from Scrapbook in that it is designed to capture notes and sketches using the S Pen, rather than snippets of already-existing content from the Internet or other apps. In other words, Scrapbooker is like a real-life scrapbook, while S Note is like a blank pad of paper. However, S Note is much more than that, as it offers handwriting recognition, shape and chart creation tools, and more.

- **Easy Clip**: Easy Clip is a special tool used with the Scrapbook to neatly crop portions of images. For example, when selecting content to include in your Scrapbook, you can trace the outline of an object in a photograph, and Easy Clip will tidy up your lines so that you get a clean result, with the background stripped out.

- **Pen Window**: Pen Window allows you to quickly call up a foreground mini-window in which to run another app, leaving your current app accessible in the background. The size and placement of the Pen Window can be easily controlled; you simply draw a rectangle to specify the size and position.

- **Multi Window**: Multi Window is similar to Pen Window, but splits the screen into two side-by-side parts rather than overlaying one app on another. Both Pen Window and Multi Window are designed to allow multitasking; they just do so in slightly different ways.

And, of course, the vivid 5.7" full HD Super AMOLED screen is a distinguishing feature of the Note 3 by itself. Even if a user has no intention of taking advantage of the Note 3's S Pen features, it still stands out from other Android phones simply because its screen is much larger than most of the competition. There are larger devices—for example, the Samsung Galaxy Mega 6.3—but the Note 3 is still a top dog and is a much higher-end device overall.

*TIP: Most of these features are discussed in **Chapter 6** (p. 182).*

Chapter 3: Getting Started

Note 3 Anatomy

The photos below show the anatomy of the Note 3.

IR Port

Rear Camera
& Flash

Back Cover
Release

S Pen
Silo

Speaker

USB/Charging
Port

Physically Preparing The Note 3

The first step in setting up your new Note 3 is to physically prepare the device. Upon opening the box, the Note 3 may have come with a plastic film over the screen. Leave this on for the time being, as the Note 3 will be spending some time face down on its screen. Unwrap the battery that comes with your Note 3.

Find a smooth surface and place the Note 3 with its screen facing down. As you will see, the back case has been designed to mimic leather, and even has faux stitching around the edges. (On that note, take a minute to observe the sides of the device, which are grooved. Samsung claims that this is to mimic the feeling of a paper notepad in your hand. Accurate? You decide.)

Remove the back case by placing your fingernail in the groove on the upper-right-hand side of the device, near the power button. (Denoted "Back Cover Release" in the image above.) The back case should begin to pop up fairly easily, allowing you to work your finger around the edges and remove it completely. The plastic is quite flexible and for the most part you don't need to worry about breaking it, but at the same time, you should not have to use a great deal of force. If you have trouble removing the back case, make sure that you are starting from the correct groove.

After you have successfully removed the back case, you will need to insert from 1 to 3 components. These include:

- **Battery**

- **SIM card**, if you are on a GSM network such as T-Mobile or AT&T. Your SIM card contains your account information. If you are on Sprint, Verizon, or another CDMA network, your Note 3 will neither need nor accept a SIM card, and instead you will need to call your carrier or take your Note 3 into a retail location to activate it.

- **Micro SD card**, if you have one. Whereas a SIM card stores your cellular account information, a Micro SD card stores data such as photos, apps, music, videos, and so on, and can be used regardless of your carrier. Because the Note 3 has such a large built-in storage capacity (32 GB on the base model), a Micro SD card is less of a necessity now than it was a few years ago, when phones had 1 GB or less of built-in storage. Nevertheless, Micro SD cards are inexpensive (less than $1/GB) and can be useful if you plan to store a lot of media on your Note 3, or if you want to store backups of your data. See Chapter 11, Accessorizing, for more information.

The photo, below, demonstrates the correct way to insert each of these components.

Initial Software Setup

After you have completed this process and firmly snapped the back case into place, you can remove the plastic film from the device's screen, and plug it in using the supplied power adapter and cable. An orange LED light on the front upper-left-hand side of the Note 3 will illuminate to indicate the device is charging. Turn the Note 3 on by pressing and holding the power button on the right-hand edge of the device. After the device powers up for the first time, you will be greeted by this screen:

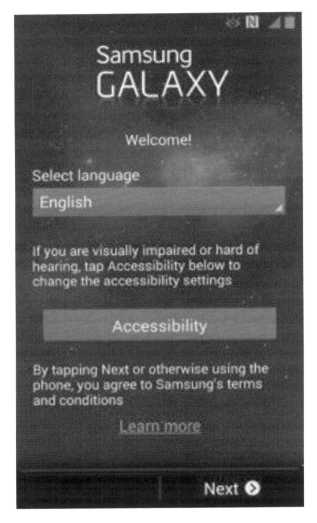

Tap "Next," and you will be presented with a message that says, "To see available networks, turn on Wi-Fi."

If you have a Wi-Fi connection available, tap the On-Off button in the upper-right-hand corner of the screen, select your network, and enter your password to connect. If you do not have a Wi-Fi connection available, simply tap "Next" and the phone will use your carrier's wireless data connection instead, although it may take several minutes for your device to connect to the cellular network for the first time. Note that this may cost you money or use up your data quota, depending on how your phone's data plan is configured with your carrier. I recommend using Wi-Fi when possible.

My router is named "dlink," so from this screen I tapped the "dlink" entry, resulting in the prompt below:

Enter your network password and tap "Connect." Upon doing so, your phone will take a few seconds to register itself on your wireless router.

Here, I have successfully connected to the "dlink" network. Once your Note 3 has connected, tap "Next."

Next, you will be presented with a chance to create a Samsung account, which provides various services and enhancements to Samsung applications included on your phone. To do so, tap "Create new account" and fill in your e-mail address, password, date of birth, and other information. The process is optional. Personally, I do not use a Samsung account, because a Google account already does nearly everything a Samsung account does, and a Samsung account requires additional, battery-draining account syncing. (The most significant benefit of a Samsung account is text message backup, but you can accomplish that through Kies. (p.252))

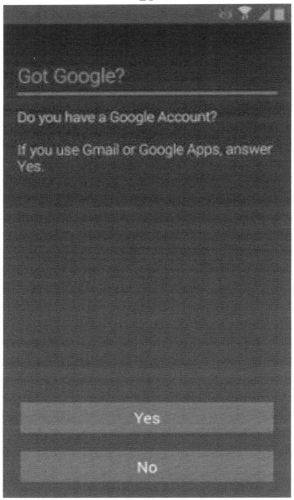

Next, you will be prompted to sign into your existing Google account or create a new one, if you do not have one already. This is an absolute must; the entire Android OS is built around the Google ecosystem, and you will miss out on a huge number of features if you do not connect your Google account to your Note 3. For example, you will not be able to use the built-in Gmail app, you will not be able to sync and backup your contacts, you will not be able to sync your bookmarks and passwords through Chrome, and critically, you will not be able to download any new apps from the Google Play Store. So, either tap "Yes" and sign into your account, or click "No" and follow the instructions to create a new Google account.

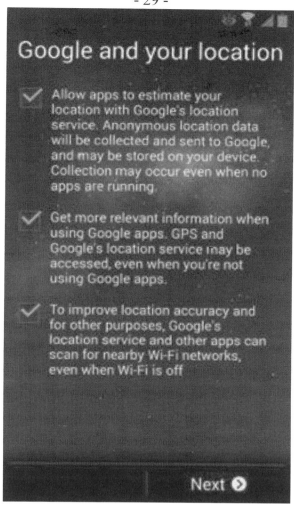

After you have created or signed into your Google account, you will have the opportunity to configure some privacy settings, as shown in the screenshot, above. Although some users may perceive these settings to be invasive, the truth is that Google has no interest in snooping on your location or private affairs. They will analyze your data as a way to improve their own services and products, but in my opinion, since you bought the device you might as well take advantage of its capabilities, NSA be damned. I suggest leaving all of the location services enabled (boxes checked), in order to get the most out of local search results, Google Now, directions and route guidance through the Maps app, and so on.

Upon tapping "Next," you will have a chance to enter your first and last name. This will carry over to some applications, and may help you recover your Note 3 if you ever lose it.

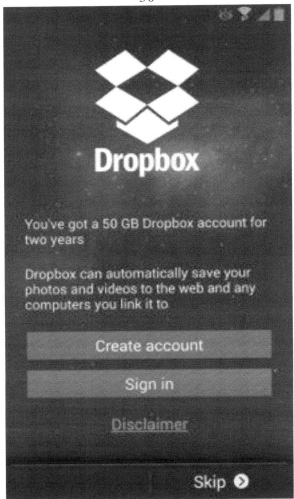

Next, you will have a chance to sign into your Dropbox account or create a new account if you do not have one. Although a Dropbox account is not quite as critical as a Google account, I very strongly recommend creating one. Dropbox is a cloud storage service, meaning it allows you to store your data on Dropbox's secure servers and access it from any number of client computers, including your Note 3, your desktop or laptop PC, your tablet if you have one, and even from a web browser on a public computer. In this way, your data is available to you no matter where you are.

In my opinion, Dropbox is a fantastic service. I store all of my work files and documents in my Dropbox, which allows me to access them from anywhere at any time—including from my Note 3—flexibility that has served me well when I have been away from my computer. Additionally, it provides a very easy way of transferring files between your PC and Note 3; just copy a file into your Dropbox from one device, and it will instantly be accessible to all your other devices.

As if these features aren't enough, Dropbox also stores every single iteration of the files you save in it, meaning that if you ever want to revert back to an old version of a document, you can easily do so. Because of this feature, you never have to worry about losing your data or incorrectly overwriting a file when you use Dropbox. Additionally, because Samsung has partnered with Dropbox, you receive 50 GB for two years—25 times the amount of storage given to normal Dropbox users. Take advantage of this opportunity and I promise you won't regret it. Either sign in, or create an account by following the instructions provided on your Note 3.

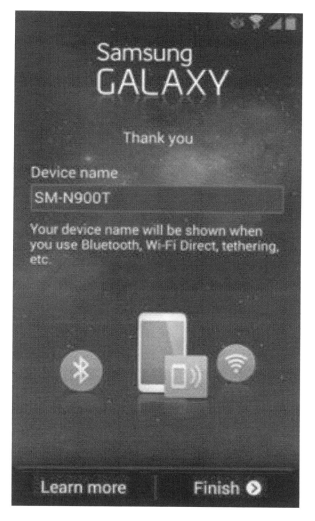

Finally, after configuring your Dropbox account, you will have a chance to name your Note 3. I suggest replacing the default name (SM-N900T) with something unique, so you can easily recognize your device when connecting via Bluetooth or when using your mobile Wi-Fi hot spot.

After naming your device, your device will work for a few moments and then bring you to a screen like this: the home screen. Congratulations—you've successfully set up your Note 3!

Chapter 4: Fundamentals For New Users

Welcome to Android. More specifically, welcome to TouchWiz, Samsung's proprietary version of the Android user interface. In general, you can think about the TouchWiz user experience in four main parts:

- The Home Screen(s)

- The Notification Panel

- The Lock Screen

- The App Drawer

These are not themselves apps; rather, they are the major parts of the TouchWiz interface itself. Almost everything you do on your Note 3 will take place in one of these areas, if not in an app itself. You can think of apps as your destinations, and these four parts of TouchWiz as the roads that get you to your destinations. In this section, I will teach you everything there is to know about these four areas of TouchWiz.

First, though, let's briefly talk about the physical controls on the Note 3.

Physical Controls

Power Button

Normally, a press of the power button simply wakes the Note 3 or puts it to sleep. I use "wake" and "sleep" instead of "on" and "off" because the Note 3 is actually powered on even when it is asleep—it has to be, in order to receive calls and other communications.

A long press of the power button brings up the following screen, from which you can power off the device completely, put it into Airplane mode, restart it, or select the sound mode. The options "Mute," "Vibrate," and "Sound" are mutually exclusive. "Mute" will prevent your Note 3 from making any noises or vibrating. "Vibrate" will permit it to vibrate, but not to make any noises using the speaker. "Sound" will allow it to vibrate as well as play sounds such as alerts and ringtones.

Volume Up/Down Buttons

Confusingly, the Note 3 has four different types of volume settings: Ringtone, Media, Notifications, and System.

- **Ringtone Volume**: The volume of audio that plays when you receive a phone call.

- **Media Volume**: The volume of audio that plays in music apps, video apps, games, etc.

- **Notification Volume**: The volume of audio alerts that play upon receiving emails, text messages, and so on.

- **System Volume**: The volume of audio for features such as the phone keypad tone, touch sounds, the S Pen attach/detach sound, and so on.

The Volume Up and Volume Down buttons only ever directly control Ringtone and Media volumes. Their functionality depends on what the Note 3 is doing at the time you press them. If it is on a system screen such as a home screen or the app drawer, the Volume Up and Volume Down buttons will adjust the ringtone volume.

You can hold Volume Up and Volume Down to rapidly increase or decrease the ringtone volume, but note that when holding Volume Down, the Note 3 will pause at vibrate mode, which is still one notch above the mute setting. You must release the Volume Down button and press it one more time to fully mute the Note 3.

If you are performing a media activity like playing a YouTube video or listening to an MP3, the Volume Up and Volume Down buttons will adjust the media volume instead of the ringtone volume.

Also, anytime you press Volume Up or Volume Down, you can tap the gear icon that appears on the screen to manually adjust *any* of the four volume levels on the Note 3, including Notification Volume and System Volume, which can't be controlled with the Volume Up and Volume Down buttons.

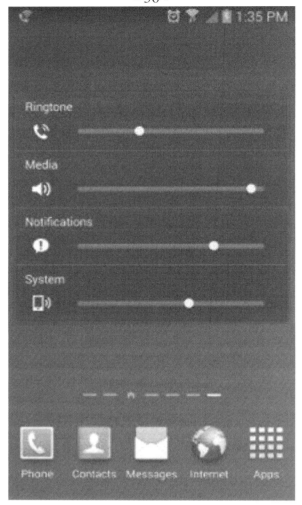

Home Button

The physical button centered below the Note 3's screen is the home button. Tapping it once will take you back to the home screen if the Note 3 is anywhere except the home screen. If you tap the home button when the Note 3 is already on the home screen, it will open My Magazine instead. You can also double-tap the home button to open S Voice. Alternatively, regardless of what screen the Note 3 is on, holding the home button will bring up the task switcher, which looks like this:

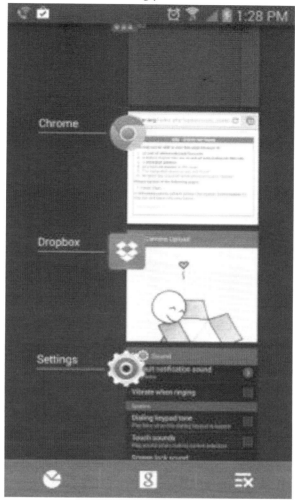

In the task switcher, you can swipe up and down to view all of your recently used apps. Tapping on one of these apps will open it; you can also close apps and free memory by swiping them left or right. I almost never do this, though; with 3GB of memory, the Note 3 almost never slows down due to a lack of RAM.

There are three buttons at the bottom of the task switcher. The leftmost button opens a system settings page that shows all active applications. The second opens Google Now (p.164). The third closes *all* active apps.

Menu and Back Buttons

The menu and back buttons are soft buttons (i.e., not physical buttons) to the left and right of the home button, respectively, and are only visible when backlit. You can tap these buttons with the S Pen if you wish; this feature is very welcome on the Note 3 after being missing on the Note 2. The menu button will bring up a menu, if one exists, for whatever app is open. The back button will generally take you to the previous screen like the back button in a web browser, although sometimes it does other things like hiding the on-screen keyboard. The best way to get the hang of the back button is just to use it.

The Home Screen(s)

Now that you are familiar with the basic controls of the Note 3, we can start to discuss its software. If you still have this screen pulled up on your Note 3, then you are on what is called the home screen.

If you don't, just press the home button! Note that your home screen may look slightly different, depending on which carrier you have and whether you have already customized it.

What Is The Home Screen?

The home screen is where everything starts on Android; you can compare it to the desktop of your home or laptop computer. However, unlike on a PC, none of the icons you'll see on the Android home screen are files. Instead, they are all app shortcuts. You may be used to saving a file on the desktop of your PC, but that is not possible on Android. Files can only be accessed from *within* apps. Another difference is that there are multiple home screens on Android. From the above screen, try swiping left and right. You will see secondary, adjacent home screens with other app shortcuts and widgets.

Components Of The Home Screen

There are many things happening on this home screen, so let's analyze them from top to bottom.

- The horizontal black area at the very top of the screen is the status bar. Starting on the right-hand side of the above screenshot and moving left is the current time, followed by the battery/charging indicator, the cell signal strength indicator, the Wi-Fi signal strength indicator, and the Smart Stay indicator. The icons on the left are all notifications. Don't worry about these yet—I will explain them in more detail later in this section.

- Below the status bar is a large widget that contains the current time, date, and local weather conditions. The Google box is yet another widget, and this one allows you to quickly perform a Google search. Widgets can be nearly any size, and contain a variety of different content. More information on widgets is coming up.

- Below the two widgets is a row of app shortcuts, including Email, Calendar, Camera, and S Note. Samsung has placed these four shortcuts on the home screen by default, but I will show you how to customize them.

- The next element is the horizontal row of symbols that includes two dashes on either side of a house. In this screenshot, the house is highlighted in white, indicating that the device is currently showing the *main* home screen. Each of the dashes represents adjacent, secondary home screens, of which you may have a maximum of six. You can switch to these secondary home screens by swiping left or right.

- Below the home screen selection indicator is the last element of the home screen: the app tray. The app tray is a special place for you to place your most important or most used app shortcuts, and unlike other app shortcuts, these stay visible on all home screens. By default, the Note 3 contains Phone, Contacts, Messages, Internet, and Apps (a special shortcut to the app drawer, which we will discuss shortly) inside the app tray.

Let's talk about how to customize the home screen. We'll start with the factory configuration:

Let's say I want to rearrange the Email, Calendar, Camera, and S Note app shortcuts. Normally, the way to do this is to tap and hold on the shortcuts one at a time, and drag them to their new location.

However, there's a bit of a problem if I want to keep the Camera shortcut on this home screen—there's nowhere else to place it! I need to free up some room first. So, instead, I will tap and hold the large date/time/weather widget, drag it up to the "Remove" bar that appears, and release it.

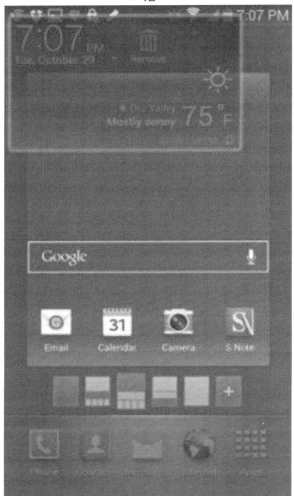

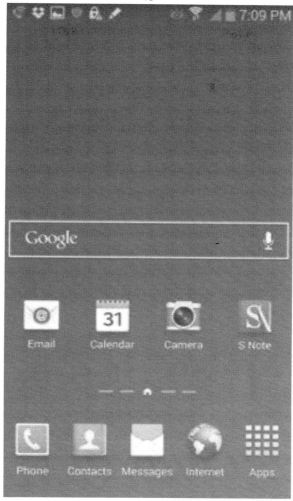

This is much better. Now, I can do some rearranging as I originally planned. I will tap and hold each of these shortcuts for approximately a second, and then move them to their desired place.

By tapping, holding, and dragging, I have rearranged the row of app shortcuts as shown.

Now, let's discuss adjacent home screens.

In the above screenshot, I have swiped to the left, and the first dash to the right of the house is now highlighted in white. This indicates that I am viewing an adjacent home screen rather than the main home screen. Depending on your carrier, by default your Note 3 will likely have other app shortcuts and widgets on its secondary home screens. As you can see in this screenshot, this home screen is blank. It originally had an S Health widget placed by default, but I removed it by tapping, holding, and dragging it over the "Remove" area, just like I did to the weather widget above.

You can cycle through the other secondary home screens by swiping left and right in the same manner. You can fill these with app shortcut and widgets of your liking, using the techniques I will show you in the next section on the app drawer.

At the bottom of the screen is the app tray, which contains five items by default: Phone, Contacts, Messages, Internet, and Apps.

What makes the app tray special? As you might have noticed, the app tray stays visible on *all* of the home screens. App shortcuts *not* in the app tray, such as the four that I rearranged on the main home screen, are only visible on their respective home screens. Thus, the app tray is the place to put your absolutely most-used apps.

You can rearrange and remove app shortcuts in the app tray in the same manner as other app shortcuts and widgets: by tapping, holding, and dragging. Adding new app shortcuts to the app tray is accomplished from the app drawer (just like adding new app shortcuts to home screens), which you will learn about shortly.

The Home Screen Menu

The last thing to know about is the home screen menu. You can pull it up by tapping the menu hardware button, which is a virtual button to the left of the physical "home" key on the front of the Note 3:

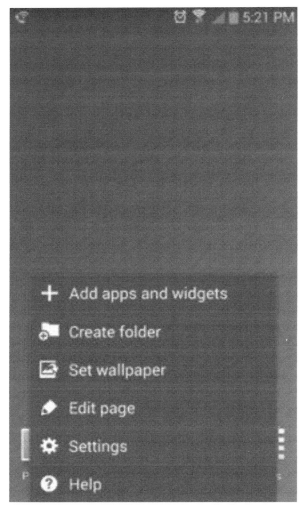

The home screen menu has six options:

- **Add Apps And Widgets**: Tapping this option will simply bring you to the app drawer, because as I will explain, the app drawer is where you go to add new app shortcuts to your home screen. It does the exact same thing as tapping the "Apps" shortcut in the app tray.

- **Create Folder**: By tapping "Create folder," you will be given the chance to name and create a folder on the home screen in which you can store other app shortcuts. Folders are useful for two reasons. First, they let you organize app shortcuts in any way you see fit. For example, you might want to create a "Work" folder on one of your home screens in which to store shortcuts to apps you use for work, in order to maintain a better separation of personal and work functions. Or, you might want to create a "News" folder in which to store multiple news apps such as the New York Times and the Washington Post, after you have downloaded them from the Google Play Store. Second, folders allow you to have more app shortcuts on any given home screen, because the folder only takes up the space of one app shortcut on the home screen, but can store multiple other app shortcuts.

- **Set Wallpaper**: This option will allow you to choose a new background image (p.180) for your home screens and/or your lock screen. Right now, I am using plain blue wallpaper, but the Note 3 comes with a variety of options and you should feel free to change it to anything that appeals to you. Note that using darker wallpaper (p.280) will increase your battery life.

- **Edit Page**: The "edit page" option will bring up the following screen. From this screen, you can rearrange your home screens (tap and drag), remove them (tap and drag to the "Remove" area), or add a new secondary, adjacent home screen by tapping the area with a plus icon inside of it. Note that if you already have the maximum number of secondary home screens on your device (six), you will not see this option.

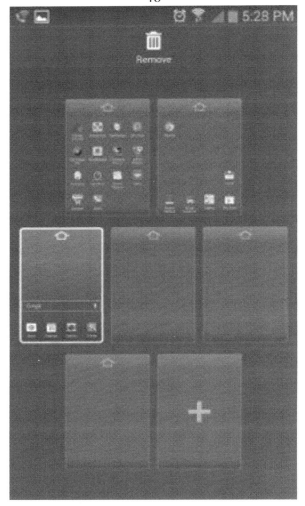

- **Settings**: This option will take you to the device settings screen for your Note 3, which contains *all* available settings for the Note 3, not just settings related to the home screen.

- **Help**: The "help" option will take you to an interactive tutorial that will teach you about various features of your Note 3. I highly recommend using the Help option in addition to this book to learn about the features of your Note 3.

The Notification Panel

Congratulations—you have now learned pretty much everything there is to know about home screens on TouchWiz. Now, I will discuss the notification panel, which is another very important component of the Note 3's user interface. Place your finger on the status bar—the black bar at the top of your Note 3's screen containing the time—and swipe down. You will reveal a screen like this:

This is called the notification panel. While the home screen(s) are dedicated to storing widgets and shortcuts for apps, the notification panel is a place where your Note 3 reports important information and provides quick access to some commonly used settings. Let's deconstruct what's going on in the notification panel, the same way we did for the home screen.

Components Of The Notification Panel

At the top of the screen is a horizontal bar that contains the current time and date as well as two buttons—a gear and a symbol made up of several squares. Tapping the gear will take you to device settings, which is the same as accessing "Settings" through the home screen menu.

The icon to the right of the gear is slightly different, and is related to the next element in the notification panel—the group of toggle buttons including Wi-Fi, GPS, Sound, Screen Rotation, and Bluetooth. Each of these buttons is called a toggle button, because it either switches a simple setting on or off, or rotates through a group of settings. For example, the Wi-Fi toggle button turns your Wi-Fi connection on or off. The Sound toggle button changes your sound settings from "Sound" (all sounds on), to "Vibrate" (sounds off; vibration on), to "Mute" (all sounds and vibration off). That said, this icon will expand the number of toggle settings available. You can also accomplish this by dragging the notification panel down with two fingers.

🌟 *TIP: You can adjust the arrangement of the toggle buttons in the notification panel by going to Device Settings → Notification Panel.*

You can also swipe the main group of toggle buttons to the left to gain access to the second row of additional toggle buttons, including Reading Mode, Blocking Mode, Power Saving, Multi Window, and Screen Mirroring without having to hit the symbol to the right of the gear. In this screenshot, I am in the process of swiping left:

Unfortunately, however, this swiping action will not access any of the additional toggle buttons in the third row and beyond.

You can also tap and hold on any of these notification toggles to open their corresponding settings page.

Below the group of toggle buttons is a brightness selector for the screen. If you check the "Auto" box, your Note 3 will automatically adjust the brightness of the screen by measuring the ambient light level of your surroundings. However, you can also control the brightness manually by moving the slider, and doing so will disable the "Auto" function if it is enabled.

Below the screen brightness selector is the main notification area. In this area, you will find notifications from apps or from the Android OS itself.

Working With Notifications

Notifications are the main way that apps communicate with you while you are not actively using them. They are very important, because they enable your Note 3 to perform valuable services in the background without your attention. For example, by default your Note 3's Messages app will create a notification every time you receive a text message. In the following screenshot, I have received a notification telling me about a text message from my friend Mike:

Most notifications do something when you tap on them; for example, tapping on this text message notification will open the Messages app and create a reply to Mike. Another example is the notification you receive after installing a new app from the Google Play Store, which will open the installed app upon tapping. Notifications generally disappear after you tap them.

You can also hit the "Clear" button to dismiss all notifications without tapping them and triggering their actions. For example, hitting "Clear" on the screen above would dismiss the text message notification without opening the Messages app. To clear a single notification without tapping it, swipe it left or right.

TIP: You can expand some notifications by placing two fingers on them and dragging down. For example, you can do this with Gmail notifications to bring up Archive and Reply buttons in the notification panel itself.

Another thing to know is that some apps will create persistent notifications, some of which have special functions built into them. For example, in the screenshot above, my carrier offers an option to make all phone calls via Wi-Fi when possible. In this case, hitting "Clear" will not remove that notification. I also use some third-party MP3 player apps that create persistent notifications with back, forward, and pause buttons.

That's everything you need to know about the notification panel. You will find that it becomes a very important part of your user experience. To close the notification panel, either swipe up from the bottom of the screen or tap the "Back" button.

The Lock Screen

The security risk involved in owning an Android smartphone is higher than ever before, because they contain so much sensitive data compared to 'dumb' phones. In the past, cellphones contained only your phone book and perhaps some text messages; today, they most likely contain your e-mail, your banking information, your passwords, and so on. The lock screen is the main security mechanism to protect your data.

When active, the lock screen prevents your Note 3 from being used, unless the user provides the appropriate authentication. Typically, the lock screen will be set to activate every time the Note 3 goes to sleep, so that a password is required every time it is woken up. The screenshot below shows the lock screen with the PIN function enabled:

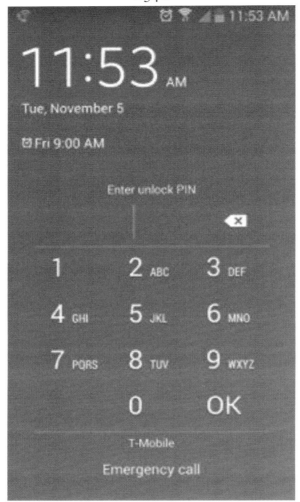

Instead of a PIN, it's also possible to use signature recognition with the S Pen, pattern recognition, or a password. For example, the screenshot below shows pattern recognition in action:

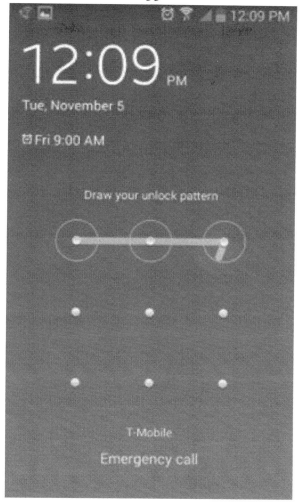

You will learn how to set up your lock screen and apply other security measures in Chapter 7. For now, just be aware that it exists.

The App Drawer

The last major part of the TouchWiz interface is the App Drawer. It contains all of the apps installed on your Note 3, including the ones installed on your Note 3 by default, as well as any third-party apps you have installed.

To open the app drawer, click the "Apps" shortcut in the app tray:

Upon doing so, you will be greeted by a screen similar to this:

By now, many of these elements will look familiar to you. At the top of the screen is the same status bar that is present on the home screen, and you can still swipe it down to reveal the notification panel. The lion's share of the screen is covered by app shortcuts, which upon being tapped will launch apps, just as they do on the home screen. At the bottom of the screen are a couple of dashes, one of which is highlighted. Similar to the home screen, this means you can swipe left and right to access additional screens. There is, however, no 'main' screen in the app drawer like there is with the home screens.

That said, there are some new elements as well, perhaps most notably the horizontal bar below the status bar that contains "Apps," "Widgets," and a down arrow. By default, the app drawer opens into the Apps tab, in which it will display as many screens as necessary to show all of the apps installed on your Note 3, whether they came with the device or were installed from other sources like the Google Play Store. Tapping the down arrow in the upper-right-hand corner of the screen will hide all apps that came with the device, and show only those that you have downloaded yourself. I discuss the Widgets tab below.

The Apps Tab

As shown in the screenshot above, the main purpose of the Apps tab is to store all of the apps installed on your device. However, there's more beneath the surface.

First, the Apps tab is where you create new app shortcuts for your home screen. When you tap and hold on an app shortcut in the app drawer, the Note 3 will display a silhouette of your home screens, and give you a chance to copy the shortcut to one of your home screens or the app tray, if it has a free slot. Here, I have tapped and held the Play Store app in the app drawer, and the Note 3 is directing me to place a shortcut on one of my home screens:

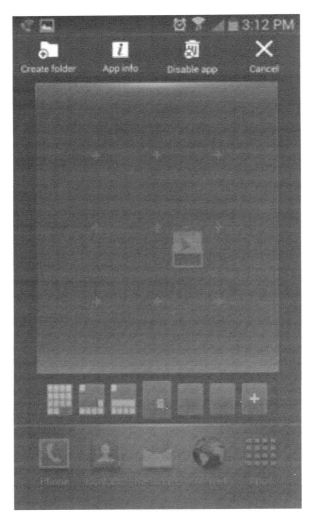

As you may recall, this action is different than what occurs when you tap and hold an app shortcut on one of your home screens—in that case, you are given a chance to move the shortcut around on your home screens, remove it altogether, or place it into a folder.

To summarize, tapping and holding in the app drawer allows you to create a new shortcut on your home screen or in the app tray. Tapping and holding on an app shortcut that is already on your home screen allows you to modify a shortcut that has already been created. The app drawer is for comprehensive access to your apps; home screens are for your most-used apps and widgets.

Tap the menu key in the Apps tab and you will see this menu:

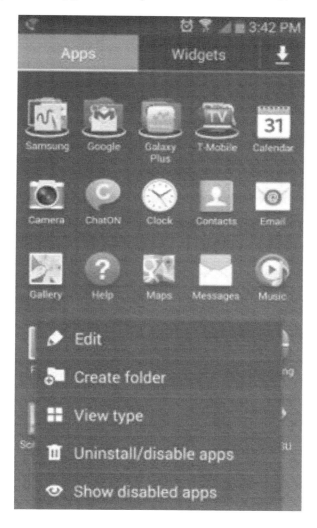

- **Edit**: This option lets you customize the app drawer in several ways. Edit mode is fairly complex and it's easy to miss options that are available to you, so read carefully.

    o   First, in edit mode you can rearrange the order of apps in the app drawer by tapping, holding, and dragging them to the desired location.

- o Second, when you tap and hold an app, you can drag and release the app over one of four options at the top of the screen: Create Folder, Create Page, App Info, and Uninstall.

    - Releasing the app over Create Folder will create a new folder in the app drawer with that app inside of it.

    - Releasing the app over Create Page will create a new page in the app drawer, with only that app on it.

    - Releasing the app over "App Info" will bring up a system page from which you can view key stats about the app, stop it, uninstall it, view its permissions, move it to your SD card, etc.

    - Releasing the app over "Uninstall" will prompt you to remove the app from your Note 3.

- o Third, you can place apps into existing folders by tapping, holding, and dragging them over an existing folder.

- o Fourth, you can edit the names and contents of existing folders by tapping them once. Once you are editing a folder, you can (1) tap on its name to rename it, (2) tap, hold, and drag apps out of it and back into the app drawer itself, (3) rearrange apps within a folder the same way you would rearrange apps in the app drawer, or (4) tap the plus sign to add additional apps to the folder.

- o Fifth, you can create a new page or remove folders by tapping, holding, and dragging folders to one of the two options that appears at the top of the screen, in much the same way as when you tap and hold an app.

- o When you are finished with Edit mode, make sure to tap "Save" in the upper right-hand corner of the screen, or you will lose all of your changes.

- **Create Folder**: This option creates a new folder and prompts you to enter a name for it. It will also contain a small plus sign, and upon tapping it you will have a chance to select each of the apps you wish to place in the new folder by tapping and selecting them. Only tap the "OK" button once you have entered a name and selected the apps you wish to place in the folder. If you accidentally create a folder with the wrong name or the wrong contents, you can edit it using the "Edit" option described above.

- **View Type**: This option allows you to change the way the Note 3 sorts the apps in the app drawer. The default is "Customizable Grid," which you can change to "Alphabetical Grid" or "Alphabetical List." Experiment with these and choose the one you like best. Personally, I like Alphabetical Grid because it makes it very easy to find apps. Note that if you choose Alphabetical Grid, you lose the option to rearrange apps manually in Edit mode (they become fixed in alphabetical order instead). Also, in Alphabetical List mode, you lose the ability to rearrange apps as well as to create and use folders.

- **Uninstall/Disable Apps**: This option brings up a screen that looks similar to the Edit window, except the only action available is to tap the minus sign on each app to remove it from your Note 3 (for third-party apps downloaded from the Play Store) or disable it (for apps that come with the Note 3). It is worth noting that not all apps that come with the Note 3 can be disabled; Samsung has chosen to make some, such as Flipboard, permanent. Rooted users, however, can even remove permanent apps (p.269).

- **Show Disabled Apps**: If you have disabled any apps on your Note 3 using the above option, you can view and re-enable them from this screen.

Working With Widgets

In the same way that the "Apps" mode of the app drawer is a repository for all of the apps installed on your Note 3, the "Widgets" option is a repository for all of the widgets that you can create on your home screen(s). The "Widgets" mode is slightly different than the "Apps" mode, however. The apps in "Apps" mode can be launched just the same way they can be launched after you have created a shortcut to them on your home screen. The widgets in the "Widgets" mode, however, are non-functional. They are only placeholders that represent the Widgets you can add to your home screen.

Thus, you might choose to launch apps via your home screen or the apps drawer— for example, you might use the latter for apps that you rarely use and for which you do not want a shortcut on your home screen. However, the same is not true of widgets. You will *only* use widgets on your home screen. The "Widgets" mode of the app drawer is just a place that stores all the possible widgets you can create for use on your home screen.

I know this may sound confusing, but it is easy enough once you begin to use the Note 3.

Your Widgets mode in the app drawer will look something like this. Note that the Widgets mode also has dashes at the bottom of the screen to indicate you can swipe left and right to access other pages of widgets.

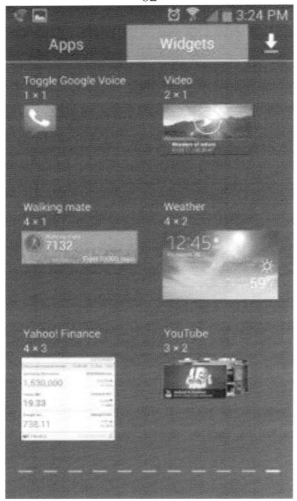

As you might have guessed from the vast number of pages available, the Note 3 comes with several dozen widgets by default, from clocks to stock tickers to weather and news.

You can add widgets to your home screen by tapping and holding, the exact same way you tap and hold apps in the "Apps" tab to add them to your home screen. Feel free to experiment and see what is most useful for you. Also note that some third-party apps come with widgets. For example, I have a third-party app from the Play Store that allows me to toggle the camera flash LED on, to use it like a flashlight. When installed, this app adds a new widget to the "Widgets" mode of the app drawer, which can be added to the home screen to act as a fast flashlight toggle. Anytime you install a new app, check the Widgets mode of the app drawer to see whether it has added a new and useful widget to your collection. If it has, and you want to try it, just tap and drag to create a copy of the widget on your home screen.

Tap the menu key while in the Widgets tab and you will see this menu:

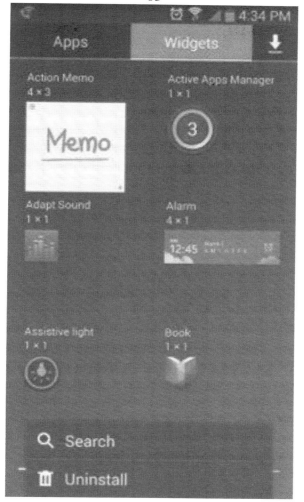

- **Search**: This option will let you filter displayed widgets by name. For example, if you type in "alarm," you will see only widgets that have "alarm" in their title. To exit search mode, tap the back key. (You may need to tap it twice if the on-screen keyboard is active—once to close the keyboard and again to close search mode.)

- **Uninstall**: This option will let you remove third-party widgets from your Note 3. Removable widgets will have a red minus sign next to them, which you must tap to uninstall them. Widgets that come with the Note 3 cannot be uninstalled, and there will be no minus sign next to them.

The Downloaded Apps Tab

Tapping the down arrow to the right of the Widgets tab is almost the same as the Apps tab, but instead of showing all the applications on your Note 3, it only shows apps you've installed yourself. All the apps that came pre-installed with the Note 3 will be hidden. In practice, it's not a particularly useful option.

Tapping the menu button in this tab gives you only one option: Uninstall. This works almost exactly the same as the "Uninstall/Disable Apps" menu option in the "Apps" mode of the app drawer, except all apps can be uninstalled. After all, the downloaded apps mode shows only apps that you have downloaded from the Google Play Store—and you can always remove those.

Moving Your Data From Another Phone

For Note 3 users, the single best way to move your data from another phone is Samsung's new Smart Switch program. It runs on both Windows and Mac OS, and allows you to transfer your data from an iPhone, a BlackBerry, or any LG, Nokia, or Samsung phone.

Download the software here: http://www.samsung.com/us/smart-switch/

Install it on your computer using the installation instructions if necessary (http://www.samsung.com/us/smart-switch/Smart_Switch_Install_Instructions.pdf), start the program, and let it guide you through the process, which is quite painless.

TIP: If you're transferring your data from another Samsung Galaxy device, you don't even need the desktop software. Just install the Samsung Smart Switch Mobile app from the Play Store on both devices and follow the instructions.

Chapter 5: Basic Functions

So far, you have learned the basics of the TouchWiz interface: the home screen, the notification panel, the lock screen, and the app drawer. Now, I'll show you how to perform some basic functions such as making phone calls, sending text messages, browsing the Internet, taking pictures and video, and more.

Landscape Mode

Landscape Mode works in pretty much every app—just not on the home screen, app drawer, notification panel, or lock screen. (I don't have an explanation for Samsung's decision on this one.) When you're in an app, just flip your Note 3 sideways and it will automatically enter landscape mode.

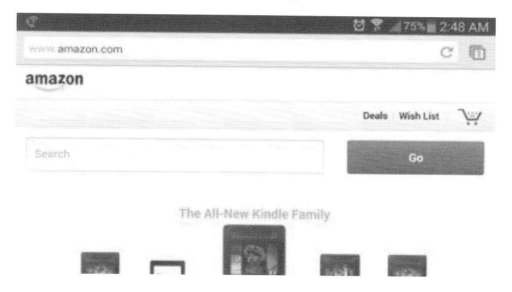

Entering Text

Inputting text is one of the basic functions you need to know. There are three main ways to do so: using a keyboard, using the S Pen, and using your voice.

Typing With The Keyboard, And Swiping For Speed

The default input method for the Note 3 is the Samsung keyboard. In the Android ecosystem, there are a variety of different keyboards. For example, you can download the official Google Android keyboard from the Google Play Store, and alternatives such as Swype. In my opinion, however, the Samsung keyboard included with the Note 3 is among the very best. It is fast, accurate, includes shortcuts to other features such as handwriting recognition mode, and crucially, includes a row of number keys accessible *without* hitting another key. This may sound like an insignificant feature, but it is incredibly convenient in day-to-day use. The Samsung keyboard looks like this:

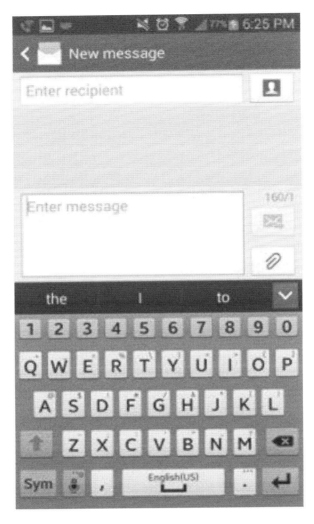

⭐ *TIP: It is also possible to connect external keyboards to the Note 3, which I discuss in Chapter 11, Accessorizing.*

There are several important things to know about the Samsung keyboard:

- Tap the shift key to cycle through lowercase, uppercase, and caps lock.

- Tap and hold on any character key to bring up the secondary characters displayed in tiny type on each key. Many keys have multiple secondary characters available.

- Tap the "Sym" key to switch between the standard keyboard and symbols.

- As you type, the Note 3 will predict words in the black bar above the keyboard. Tap any word to autocomplete the word you are typing. This can save a lot of tapping.

- Tap the microphone key to the immediate right of the "Sym" key to activate voice input (discussed below), or tap and hold it to change keyboard modes:

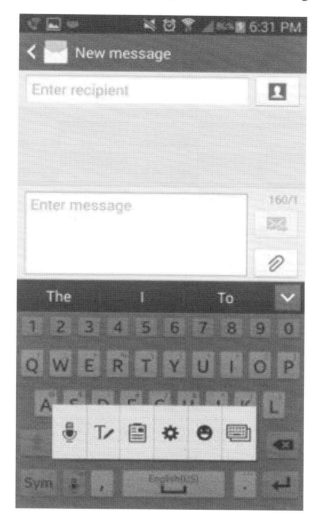

From left to right, these options include:

- Activate Voice Input (same as tapping the microphone key once)

- Activate Handwriting Recognition Mode

- Show Recent Clipboard Items

- Samsung Keyboard Settings (same as going to Settings → Controls → Language and input → Gear icon next to Samsung keyboard)

- Emoticons

- Keyboard Type

  - Normal

  - Floating

  - One-Handed

Obviously, you can input text using the Samsung keyboard by tapping/pecking as you would on a normal keyboard. You can use either a finger or the S Pen to do so. However, there is another way to type: by swiping.

The third-party keyboard called Swype was one of the first, if not *the* first keyboard to offer typing by swiping. I avoided it for a long time, but once I tried it, I never went back. I suggest you train yourself to type by swiping, as it is much faster and easier than tapping/pecking.

So how does typing by swiping work? Place your finger on the first character of the word you want, and simply move from letter to letter without letting your finger up. The Note 3 will trace the path of your finger in blue. Here, I have typed "Hello":

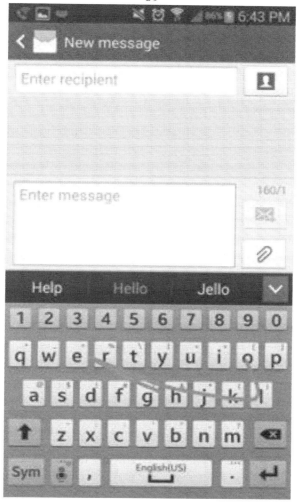

It may take some time to get used to, but in my opinion, it is well worth the learning curve. You can swipe using your finger or your S Pen.

⭐ *TIP: On the Note 3, you can even type multiple words by swiping, without lifting your finger. Simply move your finger over the spacebar in between words. This feature was not included on the Note 2.*

You can access and change settings for the Samsung keyboard by tapping and holding the microphone key and then tapping the gear icon, or by going to Settings → Controls → Language and Input → Gear icon next to Samsung keyboard. There are many options available to customize features such as auto-prediction and auto-punctuation.

Handwriting Recognition With The S Pen

You can also input text into your Note 3 using handwriting recognition in conjunction with the S Pen. This option is available anywhere keyboard input is possible. To enable it, tap and hold the settings button to the right of the "Sym" key on the Samsung keyboard, and tap the T (the second icon from left):

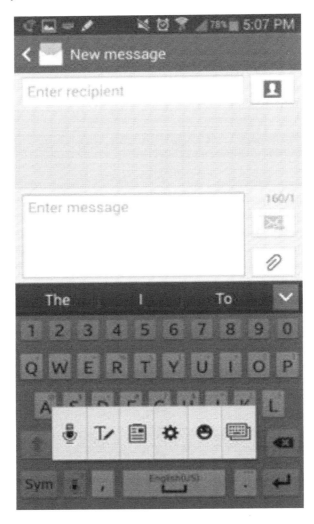

Doing so will reveal the handwriting input pad:

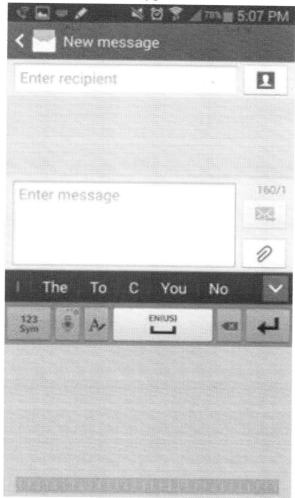

⭐ *TIP: You can have the Note 3 automatically change the Samsung keyboard to handwriting recognition mode anytime it detects the S Pen. To do so, go to Device Settings → Controls → Language and input → Gear icon next to Samsung keyboard, and select Pen detection.*

The dotted line is like a line on ruled paper; for optimum recognition accuracy, write along it. As you write, you will need to pause at the end of every line for the Note 3 to process your input. Once you have entered text, you can scroll back to make corrections by tapping, holding, and dragging left and right on the gray bar at the bottom of the screen. You can make corrections using the S Pen gestures.

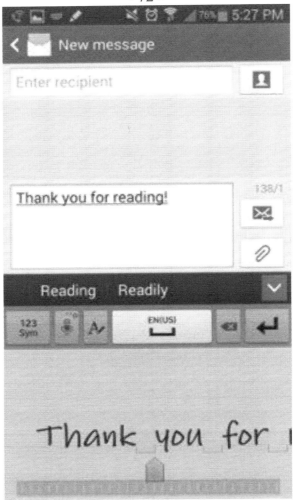

⭐ TIP: Go to Device Settings → Controls → S Pen → Direct Pen Input → Gesture Guide to see the handwriting correction and other gestures available in handwriting mode.

From left to right, the toolbar above the handwriting input area contains the following buttons:

- **Numbers & Symbols**: Pull up a panel with numbers and symbols for easy input.

- **Settings**: Tap once to enter voice recognition mode, or tap and hold to pull up the menu that allows you to switch back to keyboard mode and other modes.

- **Letter/Number Toggle**: Switch between letter and number recognition. In letter recognition mode, your Note 3 will also recognize numbers. However, in number recognition mode, it will *only* recognize numbers. Useful if you are inputting a lot of numerical data and don't want anything to be accidentally interpreted as text.

- **Space Bar**: Inserts a space at the cursor's current location.

- **Backspace**: Delete the previous character.

- **Enter**: Enter a carriage return and move to the next line.

TIP: As long as Direct Pen Input is enabled in Device Settings → Controls → S Pen, you can also enter text using handwriting recognition by hovering the S Pen over text input fields and tapping the pen icon that pops up:

Dictating Using Voice Recognition

The final way to input text into your Note 3 is to dictate to it. To activate voice input mode, bring up the Samsung keyboard and single tap the microphone key. You can begin speaking as soon as the following screen appears:

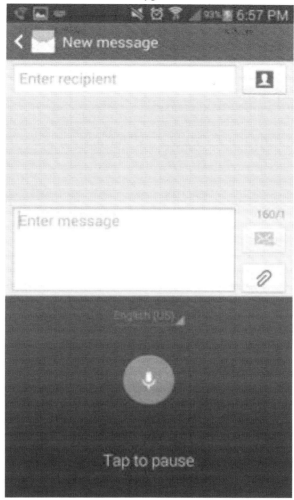

You can either tap the microphone icon to pause dictation, or tap the dropdown menu above it to change languages. When you pause dictation, you will see the following screen:

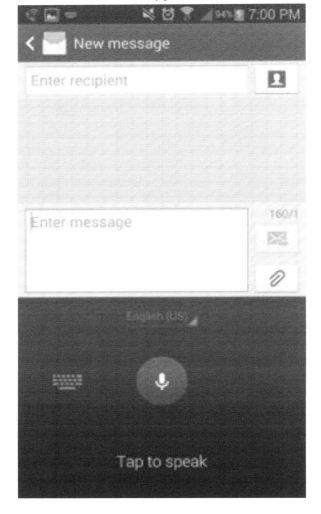

Tap the microphone to resume dictation, or tap the keyboard silhouette to return to the Samsung keyboard.

Copy And Paste

The Note 3 makes it easy to copy and paste text. First, you need to select text. Tap and hold on text in apps such as Messages, Gmail, any Internet browser, and so on:

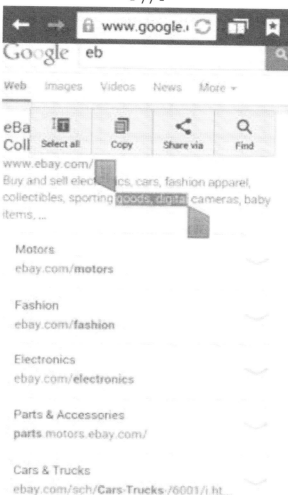

Move the blue tabs around to select the text you want, and then tap "Copy." You can also swipe left and right in this toolbar to access other options. In some apps, you may see the following copy button instead:

After you have copied your text, tap and hold in the text field you want to paste into, and then tap "Paste." Alternatively, to access data that you previously copied, tap "Clipboard" and then the data you want to paste.

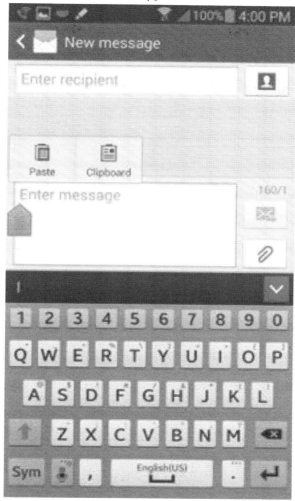

Connecting To A Wi-Fi Network

Need to connect to a wireless network at home, in an airport, in a coffee shop, etc.? Make sure Wi-Fi is enabled in the notification panel and go to Device Settings → Connections → Wi-Fi. You will see a list of available networks:

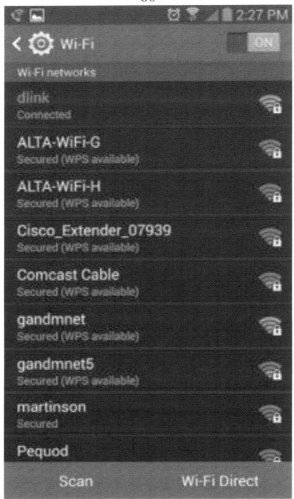

Tap on any network and follow the prompts to connect. If the network is secured, you will be asked to enter a password first. Note that the "Scan" button at the bottom of the screen is redundant, because the Note 3 refreshes the list of available networks every few seconds anyway.

You may see an entry in the list of available networks that says "Add Wi-Fi network." This option is only necessary if you are adding a network that is out of range or does not broadcast an SSID. Most users will never use this option. If your network does not appear in the list, try toggling Wi-Fi off and on again.

Note that the "Wi-Fi Direct" button is *not* for Internet access; rather, it is for connecting to certain devices such as printers and other Android phones that support the Wi-Fi Direct protocol. It is not related to connecting to a Wi-Fi network for Internet access.

TIP: For some commercial Wi-Fi hotspots, such as the ones at Starbucks, you will be able to connect to the network without a password, but after you're connected you'll need to open your browser and accept terms & conditions to browse. You may or may not receive a notification about "credentials" required. Keep an eye out.

Browsing The Internet

By default, the Note 3 comes with two Internet browsers. The first is aptly titled "Internet," and the second is the mobile version of Google Chrome. Although the stock Internet browser is not a bad piece of software, you'll want to skip it and go straight to Chrome. Chrome is updated more often, is faster, and integrates with your Google account to sync your bookmarks and open pages with your desktop computer running Chrome. Even if you don't use Chrome on your desktop computer (which you should), in my opinion it's still preferable to the stock Internet browser.

You'll find Chrome in the "Google" folder in your app drawer. If, for some reason, your Note 3 did not come with Chrome, simply download it free from the Google Play Store.

Upon opening Chrome for the first time, you'll need to accept Google's Terms of Service to continue. Do so, and then on the next screen sign in with your Google account. You'll see a help screen like the following—take the tour if you want.

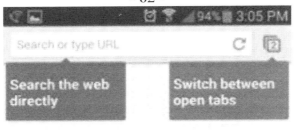

To browse the web, you can enter URLs (.com's) in the search box at the top of the screen, or simply enter words to search Google. While browsing, you can double-tap text to auto-zoom, pinch to zoom manually, copy and paste text, and tap and hold links to bring up additional options. Refresh pages using the circular arrow inside the search box.

Tabbed Browsing

You can have multiple tabs open at the same time, much like on a desktop browser. This is a convenient way to jump back and forth between web pages, or save pages for later viewing. To see your open tabs, tap the number in the upper-right-hand corner of the screen.

Tap a tab to open it, or open a new tab with the "New tab" button.

Private Browsing With Incognito Mode

Sometimes, you might want to visit web pages without leaving a trace in your history, especially since Chrome synchronizes your history and open pages with your desktop computer. I'm not judging! To do so, tap the menu key and select "New Incognito Tab." This new tab, which will have a blue background, will let you browse without permanently storing your history, cookies, or any other sign of the web pages you visit.

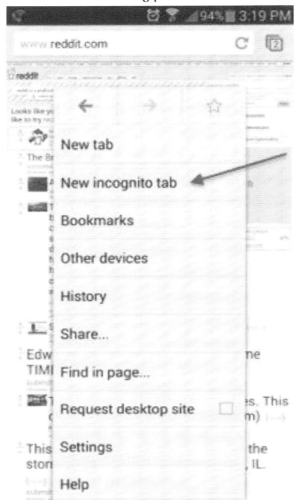

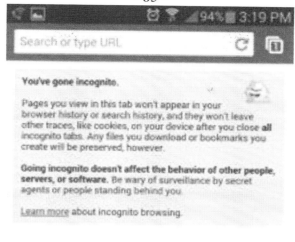

View Open Tabs On Your Desktop Computer

As long as your desktop version of Google Chrome is set to sync open tabs (in Chrome's "Advanced Sync Settings"), you can access them from anywhere using your Note 3. To do so, tap the menu key and select "Other devices." You'll see a list of devices synced with your Google account—look for your desktop computer and tap the tab you want to open it on your Note 3.

Overriding Mobile Web Themes

While some websites have great mobile versions, on others the mobile version is just a detestable, broken mess. If this happens, you can attempt to override the website's mobile theme by tapping the menu key and selecting "Request Desktop Site." This doesn't work in all cases, but usually it does.

Extensions: Nope

One very popular feature of the desktop Chrome browser is its vast library of extensions, such as ad blockers and password managers. Although there is often speculation about if and when Google will roll out extension support for the Android version of Chrome, at this time there is no way to run Chrome extensions on your Note 3.

Calls

Calls on the Note 3 are made through the Phone app. It is in your app tray and app drawer by default.

Making And Ending Calls

To place a call, tap the Phone app shortcut and then the "Keypad" tab if necessary.

Dial the outgoing number as you would on a normal phone, and then tap the green dial button below the zero key. If you make an error while entering the number, tap the light blue backspace arrow below the pound ("#") key.

There are several other ways to make calls as well:

- Tap the "Logs" tab to view recent calls, tap the contact's name, and then the green dial button.

- Tap the "Favorites" tab to view your most frequently called contacts, tap the contact's name, and then the green dial button.

- Tap the "Contacts" button to view your entire phone book, tap the contact's name, and then the green dial button.

- To speed dial a contact, see the section below entitled, "Speed Dial."

- Voice dial contacts using Google Now or S Voice.

TIP: Swipe left on any contact in your call log or Contacts to quickly text message them, or swipe right to call them.

Answering And Rejecting Calls

To answer an incoming call, tap and hold on the green phone icon, and drag it right:

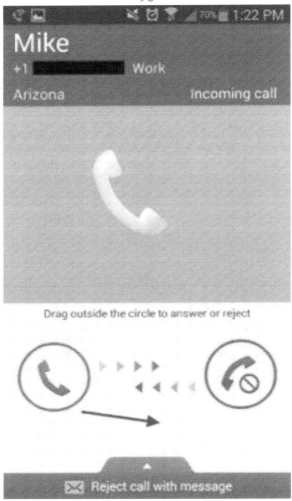

To reject an incoming call, tap and hold on the red phone icon, and drag it left:

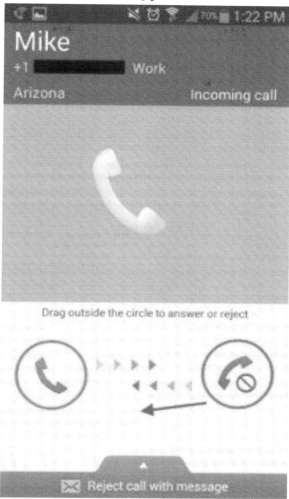

Alternatively, swipe the "Reject call with message" tab upward, and then tap a gray button next to the message you wish to send. The Note 3 will decline the call and dispatch a text message to the caller.

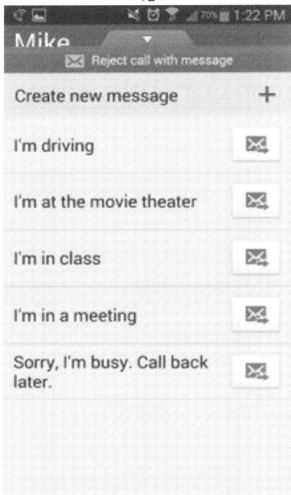

To add a custom message, tap the "Create new message" button, or go to Settings → Device → Call → Set up call rejection messages.

Screening Calls Discreetly

Sometimes, you might want to discretely reject a call—let it go to voicemail, but let it ring normally first. Obviously all you have to do is not answer—but there's a good trick to know. When the Note 3 is ringing, just tap the Volume Down key to silence the ringtone, but let the call continue to voicemail normally. This way, the caller won't think you're rejecting their call after one or two rings, and you won't have to put up with the ringtone.

Speed Dial

To create a new speed dial contact, go to the Phone app and tap the "Keypad" tab. Tap the menu button and then "Speed dial setting." From this page, tap the number to which you wish to assign a contact and select the appropriate contact/phone number.

To dial a speed dial contact, go to the Phone app and tap the "Keypad" tab. Dial the speed dial number, holding the last digit until the contact is dialed. For example, to dial the contact associated with speed dial "2," simply tap and hold 2. To dial the contact associated with speed dial "25," tap 2, then tap and hold 5.

To replace or remove a speed dial contact, go to the Phone app and tap the "Keypad" tab. Tap the menu button and then "Speed dial setting." From this page, tap and hold the contact you wish to remove or reassign, and then select the desired option and follow the prompts. You can also reorder or remove contacts by tapping the menu and then the desired option.

Checking Voicemail

To check your voicemail, go to the Phone app and tap the "Keypad" tab. Tap the cassette tape icon below the star ("*") key and follow the prompts. The first time you call your voicemail, you may need to set a PIN and greeting depending on your carrier's procedures.

Visual Voicemail

Depending on your carrier, you may have a visual voicemail app in your app drawer. This will display your voicemails in list form on the screen, rather than requiring you to listen to your voicemails and press number commands. If your carrier supports this option, try it out—it's a big step up.

Sending Text Messages And Picture Messages

Text messages on the Note 3 are sent through the Messages app. It is in your app tray and app drawer by default.

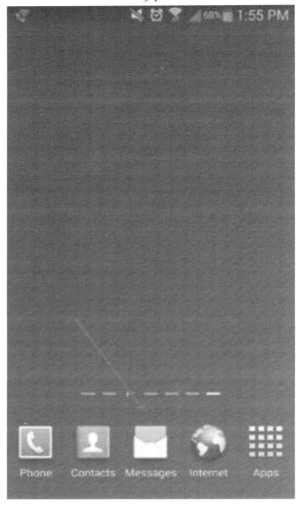

After you have opened the Messages app, tap the pen and paper icon in the upper-right-hand corner of the screen to compose a new text message.

Tap at the top of the screen to compose a message

No messages

To select a recipient, tap in the "Enter recipient" field and type a phone number or name in your contacts. Alternatively, tap the button to the right of the "Enter recipient" field and select a contact from your phone book. You can enter multiple recipients. Some carriers support group messaging, so if you include multiple recipients, any replies sent to you will also be sent to all of your original recipients. Be careful with this feature—it can be very useful, but potentially very awkward if you don't know it exists.

To enter a message, tap in the "Enter message" field and type your message. You can attach a media file (image, voice recording, etc.) by tapping the paper clip icon to the right of the "enter message" field, opening the Gallery, and selecting a picture. This is how to send a picture message, otherwise known as an MMS!

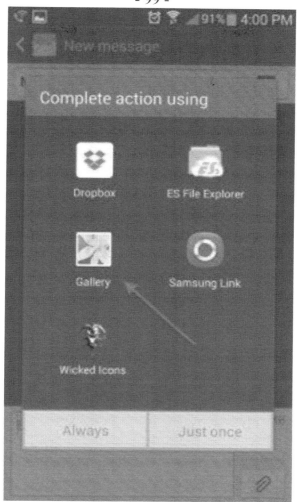

Once you have selected a recipient and composed your message, tap the envelope icon above the paper clip icon to send your message.

When you receive a response to a text message, you will receive a notification in your notification panel, as well as an orange bubble in the Messages app.

Tap the entry in your Messages app, or in your notification panel to open the thread.

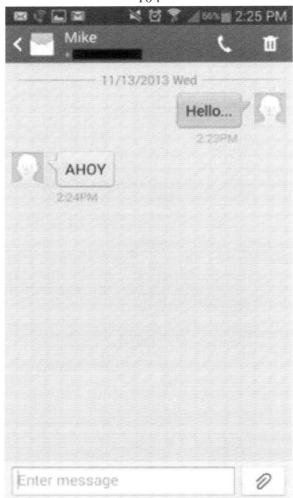

Compose further replies in the same manner as described above.

Using The Gmail App

On the Note 3, there are two apps from which you can send and receive e-mails. The first is the Gmail app, which is optimized for Gmail users. For a majority of Android users, this will probably be your only, or at least most commonly used, email app. The second option is the Email app, which is compatible with any POP3 or IMAP mailbox. You may find the Email app useful if you have a non-Gmail e-mail account that you use frequently.

Setup And The Inbox

Before you can use the Gmail app, you will need to set up a Google account on your Note 3. Most readers probably did this during initial setup, as described in Chapter 3. If you did not, launching the Gmail app will prompt you to do so. Unlike the Phone and Messages apps, the Gmail app is not in your app tray by default. You can access it by going to the app drawer and expanding the "Google" folder. I suggest creating a shortcut on your home screen or in your app tray if you plan to use Gmail extensively. Once you have configured Gmail, you will see this screen.

Let's discuss the controls available in the inbox.

- Tap on any email to open, view, and reply to it.

- Swipe an email left or right to archive it.

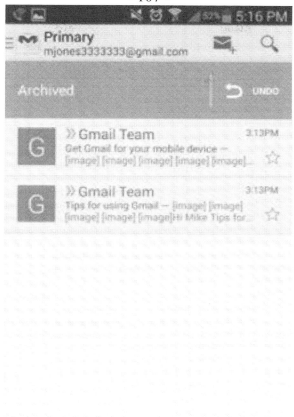

- Tap and hold an email to select it and enter selection mode. From here, you can tap and hold other emails to select them as well. Once in selection mode, use the controls along the top of the screen to choose what to do with the selected emails.

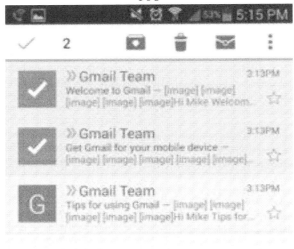

- Swipe from the left side of the screen right, or tap the red envelope in the upper-left-hand corner of the screen to pull up the toolbar. From here, you can swipe up and down to scroll, and tap to select the account, folder, or label you want to open.

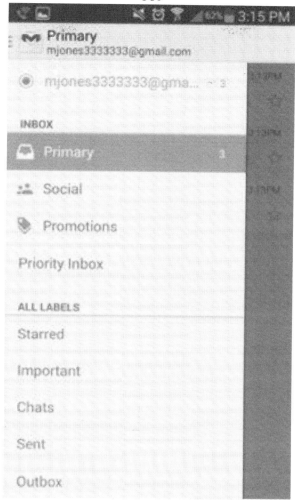

- Tap the gray envelope in the upper-right-hand corner of the screen to compose a new email.

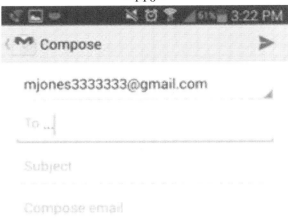

- Finally, you can tap the magnifying glass icon in the upper-right-hand corner of the screen to search your Gmail account.

Reading Emails

When reading an email, from left to right, the controls at the top of the screen include:

- Red Envelope: Back to inbox.

- Folder: Archive email.

- Trashcan: Delete email.

- Gray Envelope: Mark as unread.

Reply with the left-pointing arrow, or reply-all or forward the email with the vertical dot menu. You can also tap the tiny down carat to display sender and recipient information. Tap the purple (or other colored) letter to view and/or create a contact associated with the email's sender. You can also pinch with two fingers to zoom in and out.

Composing An Email

Upon choosing to create a new message, reply, reply-all, or forward an email, you will be presented with a composition screen:

Tap "Reply" to change the mode of your email (reply, reply-all, or forward). Below, you can add or remove recipients in the "To" field, and edit the subject if you wish. Compose your email in the composition field. The right-facing arrow in the upper-right-hand corner of the screen will send the email.

Attaching Files

To attach a picture or video file, tap the menu button and select the appropriate option. Unfortunately, it is not possible to attach files other than pictures or video from within the Gmail app. Fortunately, there is a way around this limitation (p.229).

Refreshing Your Inbox

Sometimes, the Gmail app gets backed up and stops showing new emails. If this happens, bring it back into sync by tapping the menu button in the Inbox and selecting "Refresh." Sometimes this does not fix the problem, however, and in that case you'll need to restart your Note 3. In particular, sometimes emails with large attachments get stuck in the Outbox and the only way to get them to send is to restart. These problems don't happen all the time, but often enough you should be aware of them.

Store More Emails Offline

By default, the Note 3 stores your last 30 days of messages on its internal memory. For anything older than that, it has to connect to Google's servers. If you spend a lot of time in areas without connections, consider increasing this setting in Gmail Settings → Your Account → Days Of Mail To Sync.

Get A Notification For Every New Email

By default, if you receive multiple emails in a short period of time, your Note 3 will sound a notification only the first time. This can be bad if there is an urgent chain of emails, because you might not realize you've received more than one. To make your Note 3 sound a notification for every single new email, go to Gmail Settings → Your Account → Inbox Sound & Vibrate and check "Notify For Every Message."

Disable Swipe To Archive To Prevent Accidents

As I showed you earlier, by default you can swipe an email in your inbox right or left to archive it. While this is neat, unfortunately it is far too easy to accidentally swipe a message away and miss the short window to tap "Undo." Unlike accidentally deleting an email, there is no way to know which email you archived this way! There have been many times where I accidentally archived an email that I knew was important, but couldn't figure out what it was. To prevent this, go to Gmail Settings → General Settings and disable "Swipe To Archive."

Auto-Fit Messages

To make messages conform to the screen size of your Note 3, go to Gmail Settings → General Settings and enable "Auto-Fit Messages." Without this setting enabled, you will often have to pan left and right to read emails that are wider than your screen, which is very inconvenient.

Confirm Before Sending

In a professional setting, few things are worse than sending an email you didn't mean to send. To avoid this, go to Gmail Settings → General Settings and enable "Confirm Before Sending." You'll receive a confirmation dialog every time you attempt to send a message, preventing a classic faux pas. Just make sure not to accidentally reply-all when you don't mean to.

Customize Your Inbox Categories

Google recently introduced a Gmail feature that splits your inbox into various tabs such as "Social" and "Promotional." If you detest this feature as much as I do, it's easy to switch off. Go to Gmail Settings → Your Account → Inbox Categories and uncheck the categories you don't want.

Set A Signature

To set a signature for all emails sent from your Note 3, go to Gmail Settings → Your Account → Signature.

Muting Conversations

The Gmail app includes a "muting" feature, which when set will automatically archive all future emails in a given conversation, skipping your inbox entirely. This is a great feature if you've been CC'd on an ongoing email thread you don't care about. To mute a conversation, open it, tap the menu key, and then "Mute."

Using The Email App For Non-Gmail Accounts

As I mentioned earlier, the Email app is only necessary if you frequently use a non-Gmail account. It supports all POP3 and IMAP mailboxes. If this means nothing to you, feel free to skip this section. But if you do want to set up a non-Gmail account, Email is the app you want. You will be prompted to create an account upon opening Email for the first time:

Although I have repeatedly recommended using the Gmail app for Gmail accounts, it is possible to use Email to manage Gmail accounts, and that is exactly what I am doing here for purposes of demonstration. Again, though, you would most likely use Email for work email or other non-Gmail email.

The Email app comes pre-configured with settings for a wide variety of email providers, so you can try simply entering your email address and password and clicking "Next," to attempt to automatically connect. However, you may need to manually configure Email if it does not have settings for your server. To do so, click "Manual setup" and follow the prompts. Your system administrator can provide the needed information.

Upon clicking "Next," assuming your credentials are valid, your Note 3 will briefly display a "Checking incoming server settings" followed by this screen:

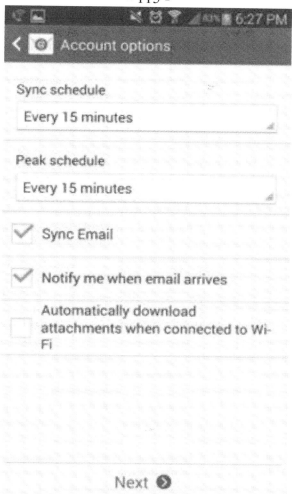

Select your desired settings (leave "Sync Email on) and click "Next."

TIP: Peak schedule" allows you to choose a different sync schedule during business hours. You can set your business/peak hours in Email → Menu → Device Settings → Account Settings → Your Account → Sync Settings → Sync Schedule.

Choose an account name and a name for outgoing emails, and click "Done" to bring up your Inbox.

Taking Photos

Photos and video are taken from the Camera app, which you will find in your app drawer. The Note 3 has a 13-megapixel rear camera with an f/2.2 lens and 1/3.06" sensor, as well as a 2-megapixel front camera.

By default, the Camera app opens into camera (as opposed to video) mode. Let's discuss the features available from this screen, starting at the bottom and moving clockwise around the screen.

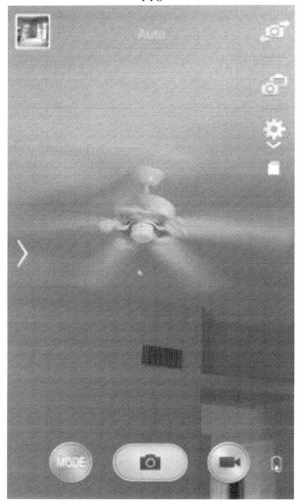

- To autofocus and take a photo, tap the shutter button (camera icon) in the center-bottom portion of the screen.

- Tap "Mode" to select from a variety of options such as panorama and HDR modes.

- Tap the right-facing white carat on the left edge of the screen to open and choose from different effects such as black & white and sepia.

- Tap the thumbnail in the upper-left-hand corner of the screen to open recently taken photos in the Gallery app.

- Tap the camera/arrow icon in the upper-right-hand corner of the screen to switch between the rear and front cameras.

- Tap the camera icon below it to use both cameras simultaneously in dual camera mode.

- Tap the gear icon to open settings (discussed below) for the camera.

- To the right of the shutter button is a video camera icon, which exits camera mode and enters video mode.

- Tap anywhere on the scene itself to change the autofocus point.

Using Burst Shot To Capture Fast Action

The Note 3 is capable of taking multiple shots in rapid succession, which is useful for fast action scenes. To enable burst shot, open the extended Camera settings as described above and change "Burst Shot" to "On."

Using Smart Stabilization/Night Mode To Improve Photo Quality

For some reason, the Note 3's smart stabilization feature is off by default. This feature digitally stabilizes the camera image to reduce blur and allow shooting in lower-light settings, and replaces the night mode of the Note 2. Since the quality of night shots is detestable with the Note 3 set to auto mode, I strongly suggest making use of this feature. To enable it, open the extended Camera settings and change "Smart Stabilization" to "On."

Tagging Your Photos With Location Data

Ever take a photo and can't remember where you took it? You can eliminate this problem using the Note 3's location tagging. It will embed GPS coordinates in the metadata of your photos. To enable it, open the extended Camera settings, tap the third tab (yet another gear icon) and change "Location tag" to "On." You'll need a program like Lightroom or other advanced image viewer to view these data. Also, if you enable this feature, remember that the GPS information will go along with any photos you post online! This feature can be useful, but be careful not to cause yourself any privacy problems by, say, distributing photos with your home's GPS coordinates embedded in them.

Using The Volume Keys As Shutter Buttons

Sometimes, tapping the screen to take a shot is clumsy. Fortunately, it's possible to set up the Volume Up and Volume Down buttons to function as shutter buttons. To do so, open the extended Camera settings, tap the third tab (the gear icon), and change "Volume Key" to "The Camera Key." You can also set them to zoom or to take video, if you wish.

Self Timer

The self-timer mode is very useful for taking group shots. To use it, open the extended Camera settings, tap the third tab (the gear icon), and change "Timer" to your preferred duration. The tricky part is taking the picture without a tripod…

Flip Front Camera Images Automatically

By default, the Note 3 takes pictures using the front camera in mirror-image mode, meaning that you will see the same image you see in a regular mirror. Of course, this is not how other people see you! To see yourself in others' eyes, enter front camera mode, open the extended Camera settings, tap the third tab (the gear icon), and change "Save As Flipped" to "On."

Save Internal Memory By Storing Photos On Your SD Card

The first time you open the Camera app with an SD card inserted you'll be prompted to switch storage to it (except for burst shots, which must be stored on internal memory because of the speed requirement). Enable this feature to prevent your RAM from getting filled with image files.

Mute The Shutter Sound

Sometimes you need to take pictures discreetly. Again, I am not judging. To disable the shutter sound, open the extended Camera settings, tap the third tab (the gear icon), and change "Shutter Sound" to "Off."

Taking Panoramic Shots

To take a panoramic shot (super-wide-angle), for example of a landscape, tap the Mode button to the left of the shutter button and swipe to the Panorama option. Tap it. Then, aim your Note 3 at the far left or right edge of the scene you want to capture. Tap the shutter button once, and then slowly move your Note 3 across the scene. Tap the stop button when you're finished, and then tap the thumbnail in the upper-left-hand corner of the screen to see your new panoramic shot. Voila! Note that you'll need to tap the Mode button again to put your Note 3 back into the default Auto mode.

Taking HDR Shots

The Note 3 has a faux-HDR mode that simulates the high-saturation, high-dynamic range shots that have recently become popular among digital photographers. To use it, put your Note 3 into HDR mode in the same way you put it in Panorama mode.

Tagging Faces With Face Detection And Buddy Photo Share

Enabling face detection helps you in a couple ways. First, it allows the Note 3 to detect and lock focus on faces, improving the quality of your photos. Second, it allows you to use Buddy Photo Share (enable in extended Camera settings → first tab (camera icon) → Face Detection). When this is enabled, every time you take a picture of a new face it will have a yellow square around it. Tap this square to select a contact from your phone book. From then on, the Note 3 will attempt to recognize that contact and tag them in future photos. This will add a menu option to the Gallery app that allows you to quickly share photos with all of the people who are tagged in them.

Taking Video

To enter video mode, tap the video camera icon in the lower-right-hand corner of the viewfinder screen.

Recording will begin as soon as you enter video mode. Tap the pause icon to pause recording, or the stop icon to stop recording and save the video. Tap the camera icon to return to camera mode. Perhaps counter-intuitively, you must be in camera mode to make changes to video settings.

Taking 4K Video

One of the selling points of the Note 3 is that it can take 4K videos for playback on the latest high-resolution TVs. But, there's no clear option to do so in the Camera app. What you need to do is open the extended Camera settings (tap the gear icon, and then the larger gear icon) and change the photo size to 3840x2160 pixels. That's 4K!

Taking Slow-Mo And Fast-Mo Video

To take slow-mo or fast-mo video, tap the settings button while in Camera mode and then the following icon:

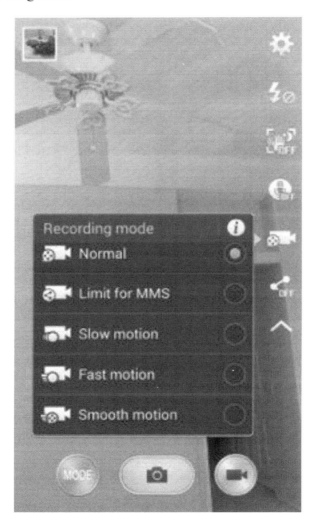

Managing Contacts

The Contacts app is your phone book. Use it to store the names, numbers, email addresses, and other contact information for your friends, family, and business contacts.

You can access the Contacts app in a couple of different ways. You'll find it in your app tray by default, and you can also access it by opening the Phone app and then tapping the Contacts tab in the upper-right-hand corner of the screen.

Swipe up and down to scroll through your contacts, or tap a letter along the right edge of the screen to skip to that section. Tap a contact to view his or her details.

Adding New Contacts

To add a new contact, tap the plus (+) icon next to the Search box, as shown in the screenshot above. You will need to select the account in which to save the contact. I strongly suggest you keep *all* contacts saved to your Google account, so they will be consolidated in one place and will be restored automatically if you ever lose your data or your Note 3. You may receive a warning message that says, "To fully sync your data, select Samsung account." Do not believe this propaganda…

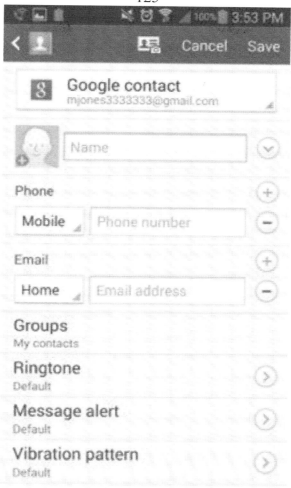

Enter the contact's information. Tap a green plus sign to add additional fields to the record, and tap the face icon to assign a photo from your Gallery to the contact. You can also change where the contact is stored by tapping the large dropdown that says "Google contact." Again, I strongly recommend you save all contacts to your Google account.

Editing Contacts

To edit a contact, tap the contact to open his or her details, and then tap the pencil icon in the upper-right-hand corner of the screen.

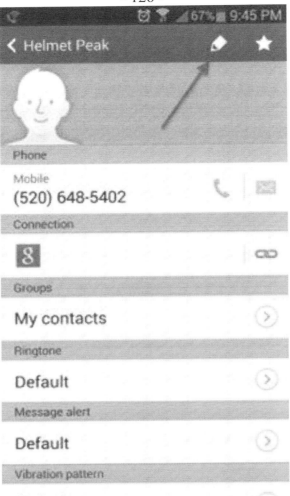

Deleting Contacts

To delete a contact, tap and hold the contact in the main list view and then tap "Delete."

Linking Duplicate Contacts

When duplicates occur in your Google contact database, you can easily merge them by opening your Gmail account on your desktop PC, opening your contacts, and using the Find & Merge Duplicates feature.

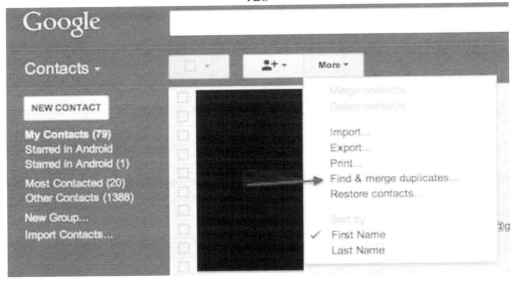

However, on your Note 3, sometimes apps like Facebook or LinkedIn will create duplicate entries. Since these are from different sources and not duplicates on Google's servers, Google's contact tools will not help you in this case. Instead, you can use the Note 3's "Link Contact" feature, which allows you to manage multiple contacts as a single contact.

To use this feature, tap and hold on a contact in your contacts list, and select "Link Contact."

Then, select the contact you want to link. Note that the original contact is the one that will continue to appear in your contact list.

To unlink contacts, open a linked contact and tap the chain-link button.

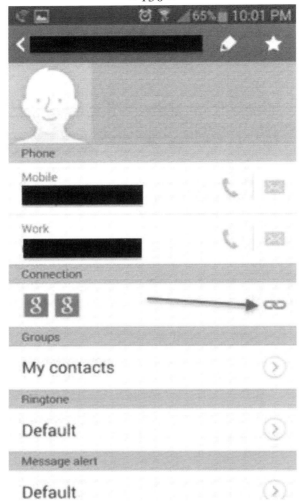

Sharing Contacts

To share a contact in the standard vCard format, tap and hold a contact in the main list view and then select "Share Via." Choose any method you wish.

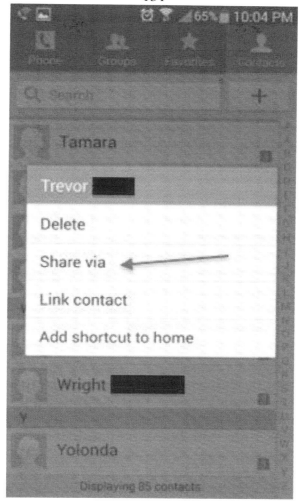

Setting Custom Ringtones For Contacts

To assign a custom ringtone for a contact, first get an MP3 file of the ringtone or song you want and copy it somewhere to your device. TinyShark Downloader, discussed in Chapter 10, is an excellent way to get songs, or see the section on transferring files from your PC (p.249).

Once you have an MP3 file on your Note 3, tap on the contact in the main list view and then tap on "Default" below the "Ringtone" pane.

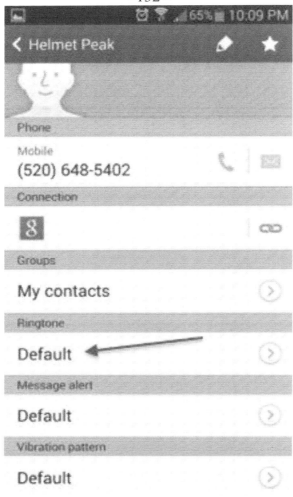

Choose to complete the first action with Media Storage and then tap "Just Once."

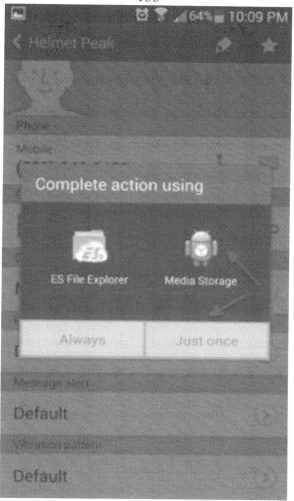

Tap "Add."

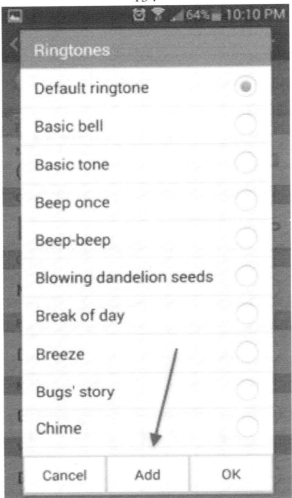

Tap "Sound Picker" and then "Just Once."

You will then be taken to the Music app and you can select any song you wish for the custom ringtone. Make your selection and then tap "Done" in the upper-right-hand corner of the screen.

TIP: If you want to edit an MP3 before you turn it into a custom ringtone, download Ringtone Maker by Big Bang, Inc. from the Google Play Store.

Importing Business Cards

The Note 3 has a very cool feature wherein you can take pictures of business cards and autofill new contact entries. To do so, create a new contact as described above and then tap the business card icon at the top of the screen:

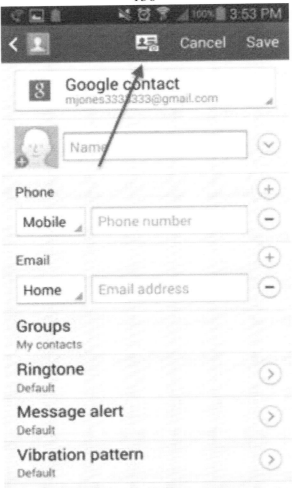

Then, snap a clear, well-lit picture of the business card, and the Note 3 will automatically fill out all the fields. This feature works quite well and most of the time will not make any mistakes, but you should still review the results manually just in case.

Merge Accounts

If you don't follow my advice about consolidating all of your contacts in your Google account and come to regret your decision, fortunately there's a fairly easy way to play catch-up. While in the main list view, tap the menu button and then "Merge Accounts." Click "Merge With Google" and all of the contacts in your contact list will be saved to your Google account if they aren't already in it.

TIP: You will find that the contents of the Contacts app have many applications on your Note 3. For example, it is integrated with the Gmail and Messages apps, so that your Note 3 can auto fill "To:"

fields. It is very helpful and worthwhile to maintain an accurate contact list.

Playing Music

There are a number of ways to play music on your Note 3. You can stream music from apps like Pandora, purchase it from Google Play or other media vendors, download it with apps like TinyShark Downloader, or just upload your existing MP3 collection to your Note 3. Feel free to follow these links for more information about the first three methods. In this section, I will focus on the last method— uploading your existing collection and listening to it with the Music app.

First, you'll want to establish a <u>USB connection with your computer</u> (p.249). Create a new folder, preferably on your SD card, entitled "Music," and copy your MP3 files directly to it. By default, the Note 3 has a "Music" folder on its internal storage, but if you have a large collection, an SD card is much better. (You can organize the files/folders in the Music folder any way you wish—the Music app categorizes MP3s using their ID3 tags, not the folder structure.) On many popular desktop music players like iTunes, you can copy your music files simply by dragging them from the program's interface into the appropriate folder on the Note 3.

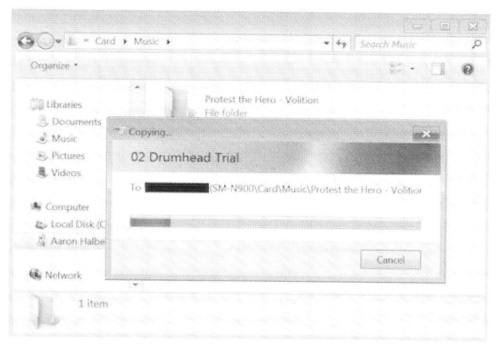

After your files are copied, simply open your Music app and your music will be ready to play:

 TIP: The Note 3's music player supports most common file formats, not just MP3s. However, if you're looking for a more full-featured music player, I recommend Play Music, which I cover in Chapter 10.

Playing Music Using Bluetooth Speakers

To play your music over Bluetooth speakers, tap the menu in the Music app and then "Via Bluetooth." The audio source will be changed, or if you haven't configured Bluetooth speakers, you will be taken to the Bluetooth settings page to add them.

Managing Playlists

To create a playlist, tap the Playlists tab at the top of the screen, tap the menu button, and then "Create Playlist." Give it a name. Then, tap the plus (+) sign to select the music you wish to add. After you have finished, tap "Done" in the upper-right-hand corner of the screen to save the new playlist. You can add new songs by tapping and holding on them and selecting "Add To Playlist," or remove songs already in the playlist by tapping and holding and selecting "Remove." Reorder songs in a playlist by opening the playlist, tapping the menu button, and then "Change Order."

Sharing Music With DLNA Devices

Using the Music app, you can play music stored on other DLNA-enabled devices on your Wi-Fi network. To do so, swipe the menu bar at the top of the screen all the way to the right, and tap "Nearby Devices." Tap on any available devices to connect.

TIP: To share your own library via DLNA, go to Device Settings → Connections and turn on "Nearby Devices."

Using The Equalizer

The Music app has a built-in equalizer called SoundAlive. To access it, tap the menu buttons while in the Music app, tap "Settings," and then "SoundAlive." The interface is a bit unconventional, so try the presets first and then fine-tune as necessary. To change the setting, tap a square on the grid and then the checkmark in the upper-right-hand corner of the screen.

Customizing Sound Output For Your Ears

The Note 3 has a very interesting and useful feature that performs a mini-hearing test to customize the Note 3's audio output to your ears and headphones. To set it up, plug in the pair of headphones you plan to use with the device, go to a quiet room, and start the process by tapping the menu button, "Settings," and turning "Adapt Sound" on. Read the instructions and tap "Start."

Note that this process tests your ability to hear different frequencies—not volumes—so listen very carefully and tap "Yes" even if you can only barely hear the beeping. Once you have completed the hearing test, you can specify whether to use the customized settings for calls, music playback, or both, as well as configure your most frequently used ear if you often use only one earbud. Make sure to try the "Preview Adapt Sound" feature to test the results—it makes a *big* difference for me, and many other users have reported favorable results.

Unfortunately, for music playback this feature only works with Samsung's stock Music app, so if you use third-party programs, you will not be able to take advantage of Adapt Sound.

Preventing Accidental Battery Drain With Music Auto-Off

It's very easy to accidentally leave music playing on the Note 3—I do it all the time after workouts. With the headphones plugged in, your battery can waste away in vain for hours. To prevent this, enable "Music Auto Off" in the Music app's settings menu.

Exiting The Music App

While the Music app is playing songs, tapping the home key will allow you to multitask while your music continues to play. To exit the app and stop all music playback, tap the menu button and then "End."

Navigating Using The GPS

Finding And Navigating To Destinations

The Note 3 in conjunction with the Maps app is an excellent co-pilot. You can get directions for driving, walking, bicycling, and public transit, and even use real-time voice and visual navigation. To do so, open the Maps app in your app drawer:

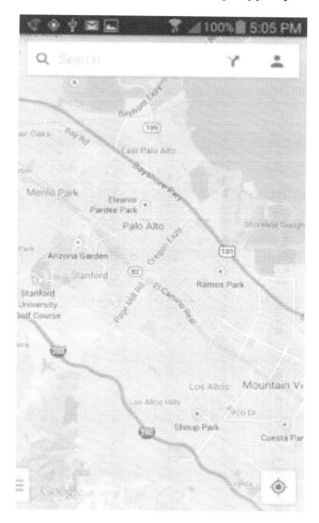

Tap the search bar at the top and type in your destination.

Tap the desired destination from the drop-down list.

Palo Alto, CA

From this screen, tap the "Route" button in the lower-right-hand corner of the screen.

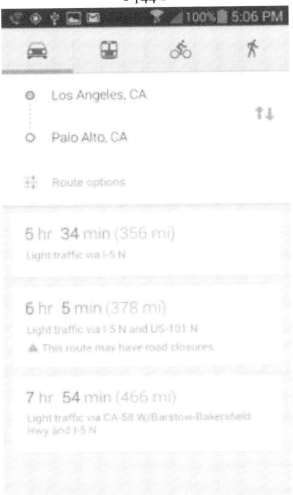

The Note 3 will prompt you to choose your mode of transportation (use toolbar at top—the options are car, public transit, bicycle, and walking, from left to right), and starting and ending destinations. It will display suggested routes at the bottom of the screen. Make any necessary changes to the locations and the mode of transportation, and then tap your preferred route.

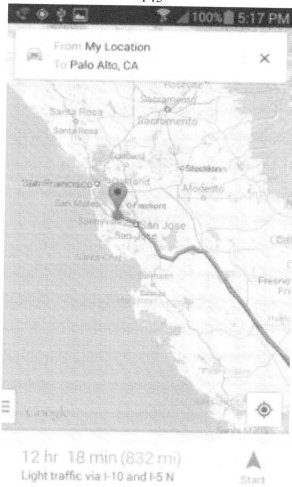

From the next screen, you can drag the bottom bar up to reveal step-by-step directions, or tap the Start button in the lower-right-hand corner of the screen to initiate voice and map guidance.

TIP: Instead of putting destinations in the Search box, you can also search for keywords. For example, search for "pizza" to find nearby pizza parlors, or "hotels" to find nearby lodging. Swipe the search results bar at the bottom of the screen left and right to view more hits and drag the results bar up to view details about a certain hit.

Grimaldi's Pizzeria

4.2 ★★★★★ 39 reviews · $ 40 min

To start navigating to a destination you have found by searching, tap the car (or walking, bicycle, or public transit) icon to the right of the establishment name.

You can also tap the list icon in the Search bar (next to the "X") to view results in list format:

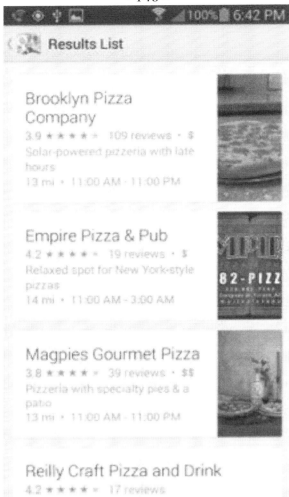

Now that you know how to set up basic navigation, let's discuss the other controls in the Maps app.

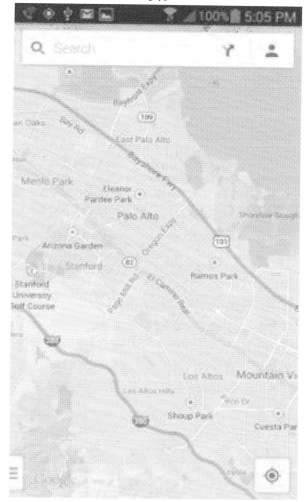

From this home screen, you can pinch to zoom or use one finger to pan around the map. Type destinations into the Search bar as described above, or tap the arrow icon on the right side of the search bar to skip straight to the directions screen.

Tap the 'head and shoulders' icon to view information about you, such as your home and work addresses, your saved places, and your recent places. Tap the compass icon in the bottom-right-hand corner of the screen to make the map jump to your present location. Tap the small tab in the lower-left-hand corner of the screen, or swipe right from the left edge of the screen to reveal the menu:

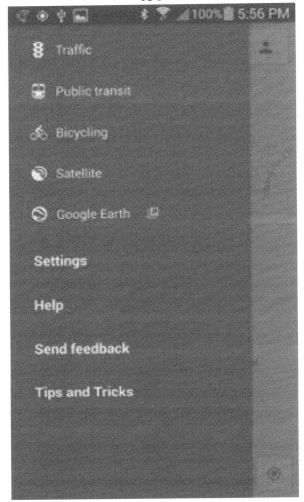

Showing Current Traffic Conditions

In real-time, Google collects live traffic data from DOT sensors installed in roads as well as from other Android users' phones. You can easily overlay this information on a map. To do so, open the toolbar as shown above and tap "Traffic." (Green = clear, yellow = some traffic, red = congested.) You'll find this data is very accurate and up-to-date!

Set Your Home And Work Locations For Easy Directions

Set your home and work addresses by opening the menu, tapping "Settings," and then "Edit Home Or Work." By doing so, you will be able to simply type "home" or "work" as starting or ending points when getting directions, rather than typing out your entire address. This is also important for Google Now to function optimally.

Improve Your Location Precision

To find your current location, Maps uses a combination of GPS, cellular, and Wi-Fi data. To make sure you're allowing Maps to take full advantage of these resources, open the menu, tap "Settings," and then "Improve Your Location." This is particularly useful if you spend a lot of time indoors, because GPS is a line-of-sight technology and is not available in many buildings.

Saving Maps For Offline Use

Google used to make it easy to save maps for offline use, but removed this setting in recent versions of Maps, presumably because they want you to be connected to the Internet as much as possible. Still, there are times when that won't be possible. Fortunately, there is a trick to save maps offline. Pull up the location you're interested in and type "OK Maps" into the search box, and search. Maps will save the current screen for offline use. Note that depending on how far you are zoomed out, it may only save major streets, so zoom and repeat the process as necessary depending on how much detail you need.

Using The Calendar

Samsung includes a custom Calendar app, which I think is better than Google Calendar (available on the Google Play Store but not included on the Note 3). Its tabbed interface is very user-friendly and the layout is intuitive. You'll find the Calendar in your app drawer.

Navigating The Interface

Upon opening Calendar, you can select from five tabs: Year, Month, Week, Day, List, and Task.

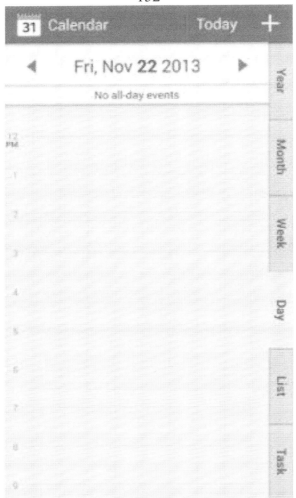

Year, Month, Week, and Day change the display to the relevant unit. I spend most of my time in the Week view, although Month and Day are often useful for "zooming" in or out of my schedule. Year does not display any actual events, and is mostly only useful for determining the day of the week for a specific date. (You can also tap any month in the Year display to jump to it in the Month display, which can be useful.) List displays your upcoming events in a sequential, text-based fashion, which has never been useful to me. The Task tab is not actually related to the Calendar; it is simply a place to keep a to-do list.

TIP: Unfortunately, there is no way to synchronize the Task list with Google Tasks. If you frequently use the task list in your Gmail account and want to sync it with your Note 3, I highly recommend the third-party GTasks app. I discuss GTasks in Chapter 10.

If you use the Calendar feature of your Gmail account, you will probably find your Calendar app pre-populated with your events—which is a good thing. If not, tap the menu button and then "Sync."

Creating A New Event

To create a new event, tap the plus sign in the upper-right-hand corner of the screen. You'll be taken to this screen:

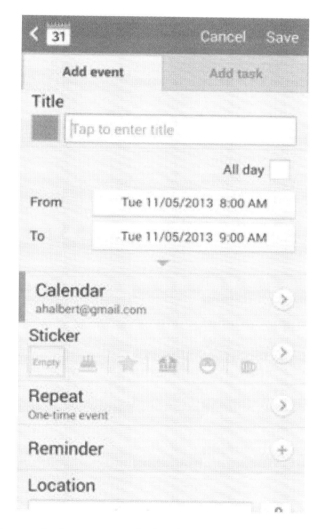

- **Title**: Color-code the event and give it a name that will appear in your calendar views.

- **All Day**: Do not give the event any specific timeframe. Note that you can still have other events overlapping with an all day event.

- **From/To**: Set the times/dates of the event.

- **Calendar**: Select which calendar to save the event to. "My Calendar" will save the event to your Note 3 without syncing it to Google. In most cases, you'll want to select the calendar with your Google email address.

- **Sticker**: Assign a sticker to the event for easier identification.

- **Repeat**: Make the event a recurring event and specify its schedule.

- **Reminder**: Set an alarm for the event. A notification-type alarm will actually sound an alarm on your Note 3 and display a popup screen. An email-type alarm will simply send an email to your Google account.

- **Location**: Enter a location name, or tap the button to the right to select a location using the Maps app.

- **Description**: Enter a note about the event.

- **Participants**: Add contacts from your Contacts list as attendees.

- **Show Me As**: Only relevant if you share your Google calendar with other people. Select how this event will be displayed for them.

- **Privacy**: Only relevant if you share your Google calendar with other people. Choose whether the event will be displayed at all on shared calendars.

Fill out the necessary information and then tap "Save."

Creating A New Task

To add a new task instead of an event, tap the "Add task" tab at the top of the screen.

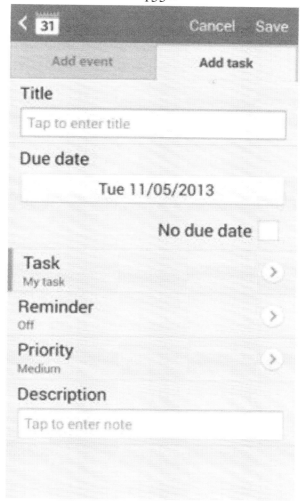

- **Title**: Give the task a name that will appear in your Task list.

- **Due Date**: Set the deadline for the task, or mark "No due date."

- **Task**: Select the task list under which to save the new task.

- **Reminder**: Set an alarm for the task. A notification-type alarm will actually sound an alarm on your Note 3 and display a popup screen. An email-type alarm will simply send an email to your Google account.

- **Priority**: Set the urgency of the task.

- **Description**: Enter a note about the task.

Managing Events And Tasks

To manage existing calendar events or tasks, tap them once in Week or Day mode. (In Month mode, you will have to tap the day first, and then the event.) This will bring you to Detail View.

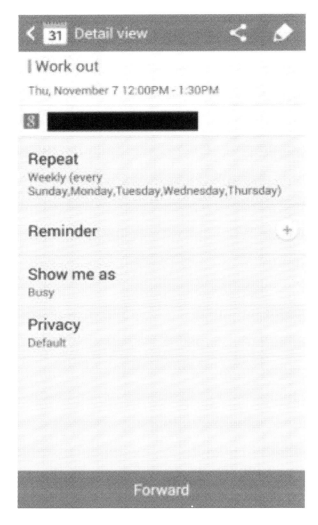

Tap the pencil icon in the upper-right-hand corner of the screen to edit the event in the same manner you create a new event. From Detail View, you can also share the event by tapping the share icon to the left of the pencil icon, or by tapping "Forward" at the bottom of the screen.

To delete or copy events, open them in Detail View, tap the menu button, and then the appropriate command.

If you receive an event invitation via email, it will appear on your calendar. Tap it to bring up the response dialog:

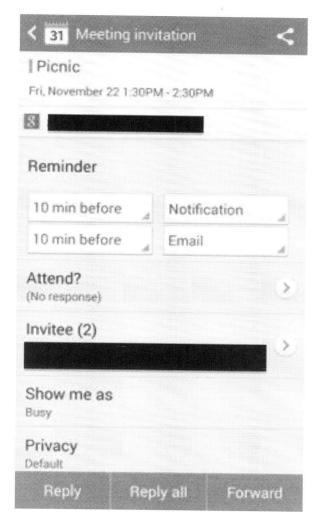

Here, you can set event details and send your response. To reply, all you have to do is tap "Attend?", select the relevant response, and tap OK. You do not even need to click "Reply" or "Reply all"—in fact, those buttons simply open a blank email to the person who invited you. This is somewhat confusing, because normally one would expect more of a confirmation that a response has been sent.

To save the details you have changed, tap the back button. (Again, seems like Samsung should have included a "Save" button, doesn't it? Oh well.)

Installing And Uninstalling Apps

One of the great benefits of the Android OS is the ability to install third-party apps to add functionality to your device. For example, I have apps for my bank, for Amazon and eBay, for reading news feeds, and so on.

Installing Apps

The best and only official source for new apps is the Google Play Store. You will find it in your app drawer as the shortcut named "Play Store."

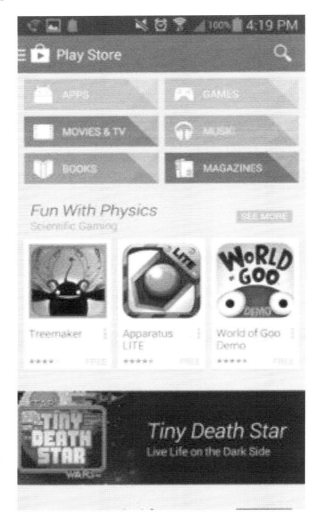

Tap the magnifying glass in the upper-right-hand corner of the screen to search for and install new apps.

Protecting Yourself From Malware And Viruses

The Google Play Store now contains more than one million apps, and some of these contain malware and viruses. There are several ways to protect yourself against these threats.

- First, stick to installing apps published by reputable companies, or apps that you have found via trusted publications.

- Second, pay attention to the number of downloads an app has. In general, apps with hundreds of thousands of downloads or more have probably been vetted thoroughly enough to be safe. This is not a guarantee, however, and many apps with fewer downloads are perfectly legitimate. It is only one of many possible indicators.

- Third, pay attention to the permissions that an app requires. You will see this information every time you initiate an app installation. Do they make sense, given the program's function? For example, if you are downloading a flashlight app that requests full network access, it would be very suspect. I always try to download apps that require minimal permissions, and permissions that make sense for what the app is supposed to do.

- Fourth, you can install antivirus software such as Lookout.

Branching Out From The Play Store

Although the Google Play Store is the largest and most common source of new apps, it is not the only one. For example, Amazon has its own app store, which must be downloaded directly from Amazon's website: http://www.amazon.com/gp/mas/get/android

When you install software from outside the Play Store (such as the Amazon App Store), you may see a notification like the following.

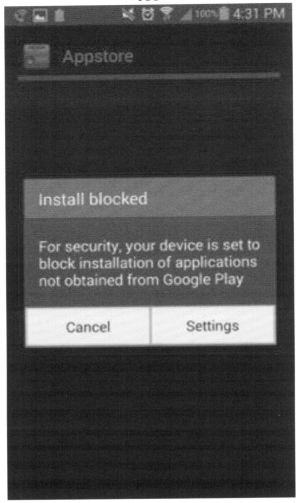

If this happens, tap "Settings" to continue.

Tap "Unknown sources" to allow your Note 3 to install applications obtained from non-Google Play Store sources.

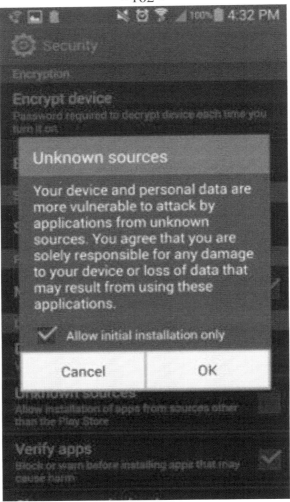

You will see this dialog box. Tap "OK." The "Allow initial installation only" checkbox is poorly worded; what it really means is that when it is checked you are giving one-time approval only. If you want to permanently allow app installations for unknown sources, uncheck this box.

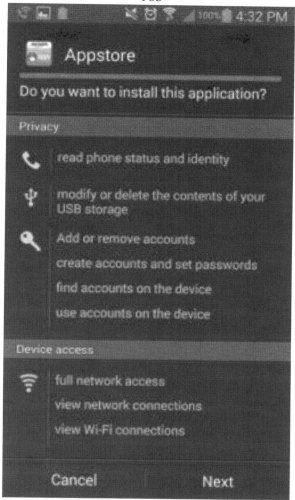

Finally, tap "Next" and follow the prompts to install the app. There are some very good programs that are not available on the Play Store, so do not be afraid to install them with this method.

TIP: It is possible to download and install applications directly from the Internet. To do so, download the file and then tap the notification in your notification panel. These files will have a .apk file extension and are installed using the same method shown above.

Uninstalling Apps

There are two ways to uninstall apps. First, you can open the Google Play Store, search for the app, and tap "Uninstall." Second, you can go to Settings → General → Application Manager. From there, tap the app you wish to uninstall and then tap "Uninstall."

The Google Play Store has a 15-minute grace period for all purchased apps. If you decide you don't want the app within 15 minutes of buying it, go back to its page in the Play Store and tap the "Refund" button. This is a great way to evaluate paid apps, as long as you're fast about it.

Google Now

What Is Google Now?

Google Now is Google's answer to Apple's Siri—a personal assistant that can intelligently interpret your voice commands. However, Google Now also includes a proactive approach to information delivery through its card system, something that Siri lacks. Using the card system, Google Now delivers information to you throughout the day that it thinks will be useful, such as traffic information, flight information, nearby events, and so on. And, the more you use Google Now, the more it learns about you and the better its prediction gets.

In this way, you can think about Google Now as two core parts: (1) proactive information delivery through the card system (information it thinks will be helpful, but that you did not directly request), and (2) reactive information delivery through the voice command system (information that you directly requested).

Accessing And Enabling Google Now

To enable Google Now, tap and hold the home button until you see a screen like this:

Tap the Google "G" button at the bottom of the screen to launch Google Now. If it is the first time you have launched it, you will see a screen like this:

Tap "Yes, I'm in" to enable Google Now, and you will proceed to the Google Now home page.

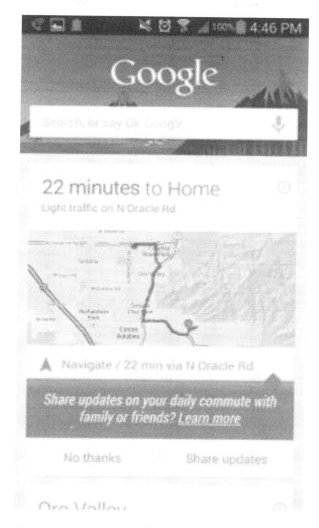

This is the Google Now home screen. I'll come back to this in a moment—but first, there are a few settings you need to check to make sure you're prepared to get the most out of Google Now.

First, make sure Web History is turned on, so that Google Now can learn your information needs from your Google searches. To do this, tap the menu key and go to Settings → Accounts & Privacy and make sure the Web History slider is on. Second, make sure that location reporting is on. Tap "Google location settings" above the Web History slider and make sure "Access location" is checked and both Location Reporting and Location History are on. Third, exit Google Now and open the Maps app. Go to Settings → Edit Home or Work and set your home and work addresses.

Now, you are ready to get the most out of Google Now.

Using Google Now

By default, you will only have a few cards such as weather and possibly commute directions. As I mentioned, the longer you use Google Now, the more it learns about you. It will monitor data streams such as your Gmail inbox and you Google web history, and add more cards as it learns about your information needs. You can accelerate this process. For example, if you run a few searches for Miami Heat scores, you will soon receive a new card with Heat scores. Alternatively, you can scroll to the bottom of the Google Now home screen and tap the magic wand icon in the lower-right-hand corner of the screen:

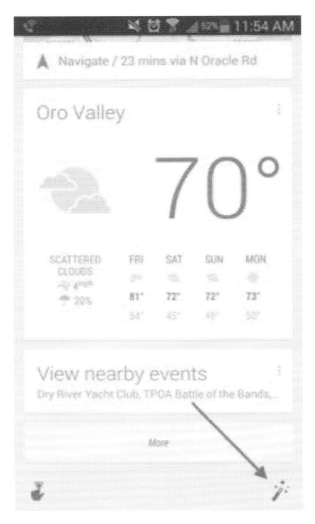

This screen will let you customize Google Now to some extent. Google does not give you total control—after all, the point is that Google Now learns about you so that you do not need to configure it—but you can accelerate the process here and expedite some cards related to transit, sports, stocks, places, and so on.

In total, Google Now has 39 different cards:

- Boarding Pass

- Activity Summary

- Next Appointment

- Traffic & Transit

- Flights

- Weather

- Restaurant Reservations

- Events

- Hotels

- Friends' Birthdays

- Your Birthday

- Packages

- Location Reminders

- Event Reminders

- Sports

- Movies

- Time Reminders

- Concerts

- Stocks

- Zillow

- Developing Story & Breaking News

- Research Topic

- New Books

- Fandango

- New Video Games

- Public Alerts

- Nearby Events

- New Albums

- Places

- Translation

- Public Transit

- Nearby Photo Spots

- Nearby Attractions

- News Topic

- Currency

- Time At Home

- New TV Episodes

- Website Update

- What To Watch

TIP: In previous versions of Google Now, it was possible to toggle individual cards on and off. Google has since removed this functionality to encourage users to 'go with the flow' and allow Google Now to automate the process.

In addition to providing useful information via cards on the Google Now home screen, Google Now will also send notifications to the notification panel for appointments, reminders, and other time-sensitive tasks that it knows about.

If you want to remove an existing card, swipe it away:

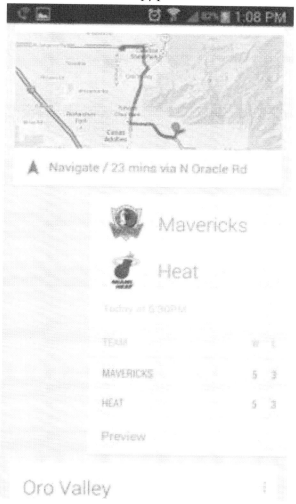

Alternatively, tap the three vertical dots in its upper-right-hand corner and tell Google Now you are no longer interested:

⭐ *TIP: Dismissing cards will not permanently remove them—it will only hide them until the next time they are updated.*

Overall, with the proactive information delivery part of Google Now (the card system), experimentation and patience are key. The best way to learn about it is to let it run for at least a week or two, see what it learns about your particular information needs, and decide whether it's ultimately useful to you.

Now, let's talk a bit about the voice command system, the reactive part of Google Now.

To prepare Google Now for a voice command, say "OK, Google" out loud anywhere in Google Now (except the menu). You will see a red microphone, indicating you can proceed with your command or inquiry:

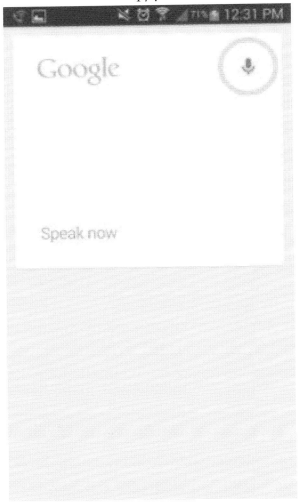

Below are the results of a couple inquiries I spoke to Google Now, and give you an idea of the types of information it can provide.

how many feet are in a mile

1 mile is

5280 feet

More info

How many feet are in a mile? - Askville

askville.amazon.com/feet-mile/AnswerVi

Dec 27, 2006 - 1 mile = 5,280 feet Sources http://

www.onlineconversion.com/length_common

htm ...

Quote by Einstein: Einstein was once

asked **how many feet** are in a ...

www.goodreads.com/.../276428-einstein-...

Einstein — 'Einstein was once asked how many feet

are in a mile Einstein's reply was I don't know, why

should I fill my ...

How many feet in a **mile?** - Yahoo!

Answers

 Web Images News MORE

Here is a list of voice commands with Google Now for you to try, to get a sense of what it can do for you.

- "Set an alarm for seven A.M."

- "Schedule a meeting at 9 A.M. Thursday morning with John from Microsoft."

- "How many Japanese yen are in three hundred U.S. dollars?"

- "Remind me to buy laundry detergent the next time I'm at Safeway."

- "Send a text message to Craig Johnson saying hello."

- "Driving directions to the nearest Safeway."

- "Call Target."

- "What time is it in London?"

- "Navigate to Yellowstone National Park."

For a full list of voice commands that is updated on a regular basis, check out this discussion thread on XDA: http://forum.xda-developers.com/showthread.php?t=1961636

Offline Speech Recognition

By default, Google Now requires an Internet connection to process voice input. If you plan to use Google Now in situations with spotty or absent data coverage, you can download the speech recognition engine to your Note 3. To do so, tap the menu button, go to the "Voice" menu, and select "Offline Speech Recognition."

Personalized Speech Recognition

Google Now can learn the nuances of your speech to hone its recognition capabilities. Although I haven't seen tremendous improvement with this feature, it certainly hasn't made recognition any worse, and Google will no doubt continue to improve it into the future. Turn this feature on by tapping the menu button, going to the "Voice" menu, and enabling "Personalized Recognition."

Share Your Commute

Remember Google Latitude, the web app that allowed you to share your location with your friends? Google Now has a similar feature built in that will automatically share the details of your commute with friends or family. If this sounds like a good idea to you—and I won't blame you if it doesn't—you can enable it by tapping the menu button, going to the "Accounts & Privacy" menu, and enabling Commute Sharing.

Privacy Concerns

Using Google Now requires a great deal of trust on the user's part, because it requires access to so much personal data. My position, however, which you will see repeated throughout this book, is that you might as well trust Google. I'm not necessarily saying Google is benevolent—just that their interest is in making money, not being Big Brother. Obviously, each user has to make his or her own decision, and enabling Google Now will allow Google to track and centralize a lot more information about you. Personally, I've made the decision to not worry about it.

Disabling Google Now

If you've had enough of Google Now and want to disable it, tap the menu button, go to "Settings," and turn off the Google Now slider. Be warned that this will reset all features, including cards you've accumulated.

S Voice: A Worthy Competitor

Samsung packages the Note 3 with a proprietary competitor to Google Now called S Voice. S Voice is surprisingly good and I suggest you try these commands in it as well. You might find that S Voice is actually a better solution for you than Google Now, especially if you don't care for the card system. In the long run, I expect Google Now to outpace S Voice because, well, it has the support of Google. But in the meantime, S Voice is no slouch.

The Share Via Tool

You'll see this feature in nearly every app on the Note 3, so you need to understand what it is. The Share Via tool looks like a tiny network with nodes:

Tapping this icon in any app allows you to send content to other apps. For example, in the above screenshot I am viewing a photo in the Gallery app. Tapping the Share Via button gives me numerous options:

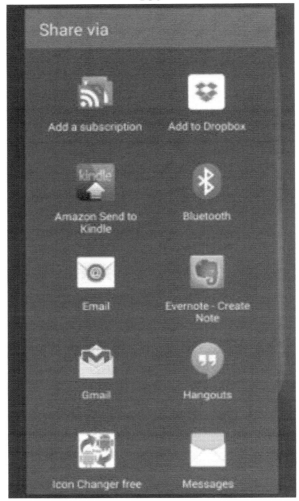

I can upload the photo to Dropbox, send it as an email attachment, send it as a picture message, and so on.

As I said, you'll see this tool all over the place once you know what it is. If you need to get a file from one app to another, chances are the Share Via tool is what you need.

Customizing Your Wallpaper

It's easy to personalize your Note 3 with a custom wallpaper for your home screen and/or lock screen. To do so, go to your home screen and tap and hold on an empty space. You will see this menu:

Tap "Set Wallpaper" and choose whether to apply it to your home screen, lock screen, or both. You can select images from your preexisting library of wallpaper, or select an image from your Gallery. If you want to use an image on the web as your wallpaper, just download it by tapping and holding in your favorite browser. You'll then be able to find it in your Gallery.

Chapter 6: Intermediate Functions, Part 1 – The S Pen

The Note 3 is an exceptional device in many ways, from its screen size to its performance. However, its S Pen support truly distinguishes it from the competition. As I discussed in Chapter 1, the S Pen is a revival of the stylus, which was the ubiquitous input device for Palms, Pocket PCs, and other handheld devices before Apple brought capacitive (finger-driven) touch screens into the mainstream with the introduction of the iPhone.

The S Pen, however, is much more than a plastic stick. It works in conjunction with a Wacom digitizer, to allow extremely precise pen input, functionality using S Pen hovering (Air View), and 1,024 levels of pressure sensitivity. In fact, the Wacom technology found in the Note 3 is also used in many professional graphics tablets.

TIP: You may notice some dead spots or weak areas for S Pen detection in the corners or along the edges of the screen, particularly in the bottom-right corner. Although undesirable, this is normal and occurs on all Note 3 units.

Anatomy

There are two main areas of interest on the S Pen: the button and the tip. You will notice that the tip of the S Pen is slightly springy; this is the mechanism by which the S Pen senses pressure. Although the S Pen is not extremely fragile, take care not to damage the tip or you may experience diminished functionality. The other notable feature of the S Pen, the S Pen button, performs different functions depending on the circumstance in which it is used. I will explain these in detail in this chapter.

TIP: Samsung also sells a full-size S Pen (http://www.amazon.com/Samsung-Galaxy-S-Pen-Stylus-Eraser/dp/B009QW3SGQ). It is essentially a larger version of the stock S Pen, but can be turned upside down and used as an eraser as well. I recommend it if you plan to use your S Pen extensively.

Features

Air Button

In a few select areas, such as the attachment icon in the Messages and Email apps, the S Pen pointer will start pulsing, indicating that Air Button is active. When you see this pulsing animation, you can single-press the S Pen button to bring up a list of recent items that can be placed into the field.

For example, single-pressing the S Pen button in the following screenshot brings up a list of recent images. Tap any of the images to attach them to your text message.

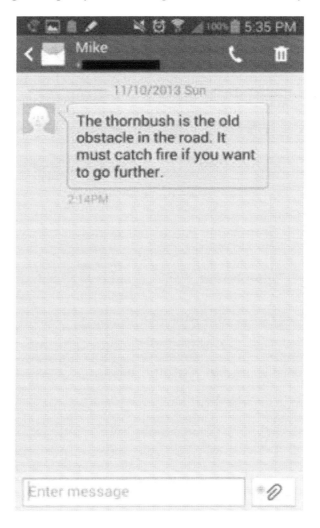

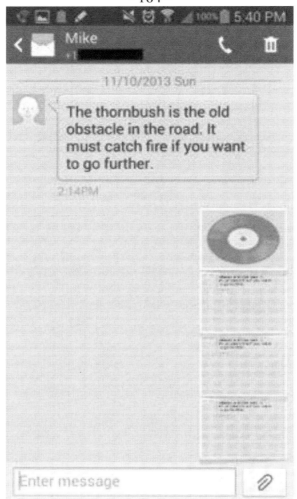

Other areas in which Air Button can be used include:

- The recipient selection button near the upper-right-hand corner of the screen in the Messages and Email apps

- The image insertion button in the bottom-left-hand corner of the screen in an active S Note

Air Command

Air Command is a quick-access menu for several common S-Pen functions. By default, it opens when you remove the S Pen from its silo, and you can also call it up by hovering the S Pen anywhere on the screen (except an active Air Button area) and single-pressing the S Pen button. Air Command looks like this:

From left to right, the options available in Air Command are:

- Action Memo

- Scrapbooker

- Screen Write

- S Finder

- Pen Window

All of these features are discussed below.

Air View

Air View is a very cool feature of the Note 3—it allows you to hover your S Pen *or* finger above certain screen elements to pop up additional information. That's right—the Note 3 can detect your finger even when you don't touch the screen. It does so using a technology from Synaptics called ClearPad®.

TIP: *If you wish to use Air View, make sure it is turned on in Device Settings → Controls → Air View.*

In this screenshot, my friend Mike has dispensed some wisdom via text, and I am hovering over it with my finger (the S Pen does exactly the same thing):

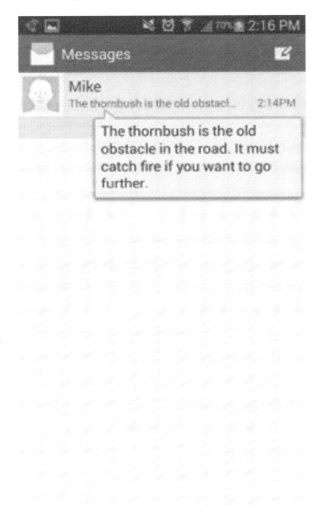

In this screenshot, Air View is displaying information about the tool I am hovering over (the eraser) in S Note:

Many of the stock apps have Air View functionality, including:

- Action Memo

- Calendar

- Contacts

- Email

- Flipboard

- Gallery

- Messages

- Music

- My Files

- S Note

- The App Drawer (try hovering over folders)

- Video

Most third-party apps are not compatible with Air View.

TIP: You can use the S Pen to mimic a mouse in the web browser, for example to use drop-down menus that normally require a mouse pointer.

Action Memo

This feature allows you to quickly write notes, which the Note 3 then interprets to execute an action. For example, you can write a name and phone number with the S Pen, and then instruction Action Memo to create a new contact based on that information. To open Action Memo, either locate its icon in the app drawer, or alternatively, double-tap the screen with the S Pen while holding the S Pen button.

In this screenshot, I have opened Action Memo and written a name and phone number. As shown by the Air View notification, I am hovering over the third icon from the left at the top of the Action Memo dialog, which looks like a dotted circle and is called "Link to action."

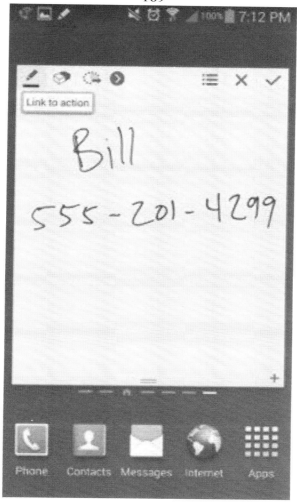

Tapping "Link to action" brings up the following toolbar:

From left to right, the options on the toolbar include:

- **Phone**: If you have written a phone number, dial it.

- **Contacts**: If you have written a name and/or other contact information, create a new contact.

- **Messages**: If you have written a phone number, create a text message to it.

- **Email**: If you have written an email address, compose an email to it.

- **Browser**: Google the text you have written.

- **Map**: Search for the text you have written in Maps.

- **Task**: Create a new task with the text you have written.

TIP: Unfortunately, it is not possible to call, text message, or email contacts already in your Note 3 by writing their names.

After using an Action Memo, you will notice a yellow square remains on your screen.

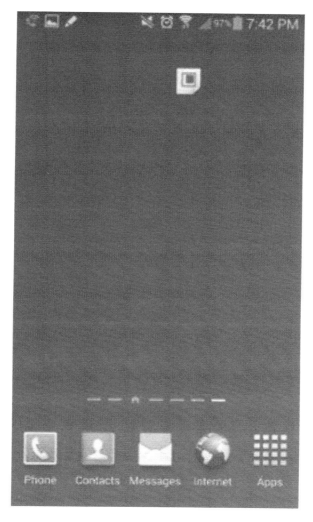

Tap this square to pull up the memo again, in order to perform another action, close it using the "X" in the upper-right-hand corner, or save it using the checkmark. You can view your saved Action Memos by opening the Action Memo app in the app drawer (in the Samsung folder) or tapping the list icon to the left of the "X."

Easy Clip

Easy Clip allows you to copy and share portions of a screen. In other words, it lets you take a selective screenshot by drawing an area on the screen. To use Easy Clip, simply hold down the S Pen button and trace the area you wish to capture. Here, I have traced Rosie the Riveter on the eBay homepage:

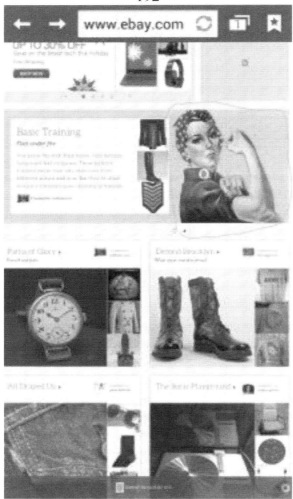

Upon releasing the S Pen, your selection will be cropped and imported into an editor:

From here, you can tap the shapes in the toolbar at the top of the screen to reshape the selection. For example, tapping the square icon cleans up my selection like this:

However, perhaps the coolest feature here is the horseshoe icon, which attempts to guess the shape you wish to extract from the image:

After you're satisfied with your selection, tap an app shortcut in the toolbar at the bottom of the screen to share the selection. For example, tapping the Messages app will create a new text message with the selection attached.

TIP: Selections shared with Easy Clip are not saved in your Gallery. If you wish to save a selection, send it to the Scrapbook first, and then share it.

Pen Window

This feature is similar to Multi Window, but provides a floating pop-up window in which to run another app, rather than splitting the screen in two discrete parts. Additionally, Pen Window scales down the resolution of the secondary app.

To use Pen Window, pull up Air Command by hovering the S Pen over the screen and single pressing the S Pen button. Tap Pen Window. Then, simply draw an oval or rectangle of the approximate size you wish the window to be; you do not need to press the S Pen button at all when doing so. Upon releasing the S Pen, you will see this prompt:

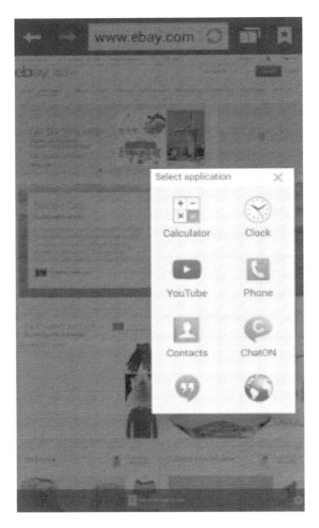

Scroll up and down in the list using the S Pen, and tap the app you wish to open. Here is an example, running the Calculator over the Internet browser:

Once a Pen Window is open, you can move it around by tapping, holding, and dragging the white bar at the top of the Pen Window. Tapping the "X" will close the Pen Window. Tapping the next icon to the left will make the Pen Window full screen (and once you close the full screen instance of the app, your Pen Window will be gone), and the leftmost icon will minimize the Pen Window to a small bubble. Tap the bubble to re-open your Pen Window.

Note that Pen Window does not support all apps—it only supports the ones shown in the prompt. However, as with Multi Window, there is a third-party app to fix this, but it requires your Note 3 to be rooted. See the sections on rooting your Note 3 (p.257) and improving Pen Window (p.273).

S Note

S Note is Samsung's note-taking app. Whereas Action Memo is meant to perform only specific actions with a few types of data, S Note is a free-for-all memo pad. When you first open S Note, you will be prompted to select a default cover style and template. Select whatever you wish to experiment with for now, because it is easy to change later. You will also be asked whether you wish to backup your notes to your Samsung Account or your Evernote account. Personally, I use Evernote on my desktop PC and on my Android, so it makes sense to consolidate my S Notes in Evernote as well. If you do not use Evernote, backing up to a Samsung Account is an acceptable alternative, although I strongly recommend Evernote.

As a final step in setting up S Note for the first time, you will be prompted to set "S Pen only mode" or "S Pen and finger mode." I always use "S Pen only mode," which I see as a great advantage of the Wacom digitizer technology in the Note 3. Because the S Pen is sensed with a different technology than your fingers, "S Pen only mode" allows you to rest your hand on the screen while writing with the S Pen, without any undesired input. This feature really shines on the Note 10.1 series, but it is quite useful on the Note 3 as well.

Here is S Note open in Edit mode with a blank template:

Let's discuss the various tools available. In the upper-left-hand corner of the screen is the main toolbar. From left to right, the buttons are:

- **Handwriting Mode**: Tap this once to enter free-form handwriting mode, in which you can doodle and sketch freely. Tap this again while it is already selected to choose the type of pen (regular pen, pencil, brush, etc.), color, and thickness. When you have configured a pen type that you really like, you can open this window and tap the icon to the left of the "X" to add it as a preset. From that point forward, you can call up the same pen by clicking on the "Preset" tab in Handwriting Mode.

- **Text Mode**: Tap this once to enter text mode, in which you can type regular characters using the keyboard. Tap it again while it is already selected to choose the font, size, formatting, and color.

- **Eraser Mode**: Tap this once to enter eraser mode. Tapping it again reveals two options: thickness and "Erase by stroke." When "Erase by stroke" is selected, the eraser will erase the entirety of any continuous stroke by simply touching it. When it is not selected, the eraser will act more like a normal eraser, removing only the portions of the ink that it overlaps. "Clear all" will erase everything on the current page.

- **Selection Mode**: Tap this once to enter selection mode, in which you can select parts of your sketch to further manipulate. Tapping it again allows you to choose from lasso or rectangle selection. Lasso selection will let you select freely, and will attempt to conform to the parts of your sketch that you want. Rectangle selection is exactly what it sounds like; you will be restricted to selecting with a rectangular selection area.

  Upon making a selection, you will see a popup window with five options. You may need to scroll right to see all of them.

  - **Properties**: In the Layout tab, you can manipulate the layering of the selected area, or resize it. In the Line tab, you can change the line thickness and/or color.

  - **Transform Into**: This option is interesting and powerful. You can transform the selected area into a shape, a formula, text, or shape + text.

    - **Shape**: Will convert the selected area into the geometrical shape that it most closely resembles.

    - **Formula**: Will convert the selected area into a properly formatted mathematical formula. Only works if the selected area is a legibly written freehand formula.

- **Text**: Engages the Note 3's handwriting recognition engine to convert freehand text into typed text.

- **Shape + Text**: Appropriate for when your note contains some freehand text as well as sketching. When using this, make a large selection that encompasses the whole note.

o **Cut**: Moves the selected area to the clipboard, removing it from the screen. To paste the cut area, tap and hold the S Pen in the desired position, and then tap "Paste."

o **Copy**: Copies the selected area to the clipboard, but does not remove it from the screen. To paste the copied area, tap and hold the S Pen in the desired position, and then tap "Paste."

o **Delete**: Deletes the selected area.

- **Undo**: Removes the last stroke entered.

- **Redo**: Replaces the last stroke entered if it has been undone.

In the upper-right-hand corner of the screen is a checkmark. This will save the current note and switch the note to view-only mode. To re-enter edit mode, tap the screen to reveal a pencil icon in the upper-right-hand corner of the screen, and tap it.

In the lower-left-hand corner of the screen is the Insert option. Tapping it will prompt you to insert any of the following types of content:

- **Voice Memo**: Record or import a voice recording.

- **Images**: Insert an image either (1) directly from the Gallery, (2) by taking a new picture with Camera, or (3) inside of a photo frame you draw.

- **Video**: Insert a video either (1) from the Video app, (2) by recording a new video with Camera, (3) by recording a new video of a predetermined size ("canvas"), or (4) from YouTube. Note that the difference between #2 and #3 is mostly academic, as you can resize a new video *after* taking it just as easily as before.

- **Easy Chart**: Create a table, a bar chart, a line chart, or a pie chart. The Note 3 will instruct you on how to customize each option.

- **Illustration**: Insert clip art or a simple shape from S Note's internal library.

- **Clipboard**: Insert a recent item from the Note 3's clipboard.

- **Scrapbook**: Insert an item from the Scrapbook app.

- **Maps**: Capture and insert a selection from the Maps app.

- **Idea Sketch**: Search for and insert various pre-drawn sketches. From the Idea Sketch screen, you can also tap the down arrow in the upper-right-hand corner of the screen to view and download additional sketches from Samsung's servers.

In the lower-center part of the screen is the page selector. You can tap the left and right buttons to switch between the pages of the note (which you can also accomplish by swiping left or right on the screen with your finger), or tap the right button while on the last page to create a new page. Tap the center button (that says something like "1/1") to view thumbnails of all the pages in the note. From this screen, you can tap the pencil icon to copy pages, delete pages, copy page from other notes, or re-index pages. When re-indexing, you must enter a name and specify a color before you can proceed. Upon doing so, you will see a thin colored line that appears on the edge of the main note screen. Hovering over it will display its name as long as Air View is turned on.

In the lower-right-hand corner of the screen are two buttons. The first, which looks like a hand, toggles between "S Pen only mode" and "S Pen and finger mode." The second, which looks like a gear, contains the following options:

- **Add Page**: Add a page to the current note. The same as tapping on the > button when already on the final page of the note.

- **Delete Page**: Delete the current page.

- **Add Tag**: Tag the current note with keywords, which you can then search for in the S Note search. Unfortunately, S Finder does not search through S Note tags.

- **Edit Index**: Index the note in the same manner described above.

- **Add Template**: Create a new page in the note with the selected template. There is no way to convert an existing page to a new template; instead, you must create a new page with the Add Template option, and copy and paste your content to the new page.

- **Background**: Set a new background for the current page, or all pages. Tap the down arrow in the upper-right-hand corner of the dialog box to download more backgrounds from Samsung's servers, or tap the picture frame icon to use your own photo.

- **Show Grid**: Overlay a grid on your note to help you sketch. The grid can be later removed by selecting the blank option in Show Grid.

You can also zoom in and out by pinching with two fingers, or tap the menu button to bring up the following options:

- **Share Via**: Save your note and select pages to export. You can export in a variety of file formats; I suggest PDF if you are sending to someone who does not have a Galaxy Note. After selecting a file format, you will be able to select the app with which you wish to share the file (Email, Messages, etc.).

- **Edit Pages**: Copy pages, delete pages, copy page from other notes, or re-index pages. When re-indexing, you must enter a name and specify a color before you can proceed. Upon doing so, you will see a thin colored line that appears on the edge of the main note screen. Hovering over it will display its name as long as Air View is turned on. You can also access Edit Pages by tapping the button in the lower-center part of the screen ("1/1" or similar) and then tapping the pencil icon.

- **Record Sketching**: Record an animated video of you sketching a note. To start or stop recording, tap the red dot. You can only have one recording per page, and if you record when you have already recorded a sketch, subsequent recordings will simply continue where the first one left off. Also, unfortunately there is no way to export recordings; you can only view them from within S Note. To do so, tap the check mark in the upper-right-hand corner of the screen to save your note and enter view mode. From there, you will see an icon in the lower-right-hand corner of the screen that looks like a pen with a play button on top of it. Tap it to play your recording. If you do not see any buttons when viewing your note, tap the center of the screen to make all controls visible.

- **Add Shortcut To Home**: Create a shortcut on your home screen to the note. If you have multiple home screens, you may have to scroll through them to find the shortcut.

- **Show/Hide Tools**: Hide or show all of the controls on the screen. You can also swipe up or down with three fingers to accomplish the same thing.

- **Save**: Save the current note.

- **Save As**: Save the current note under a new file name.

For the most part, View mode behaves very similarly to Edit mode—you just can't change the note. Change from Edit to View mode by tapping the checkmark icon in the upper-right-hand corner of the screen.

The only significant difference in View mode, other than not being able to edit your note, is that there are a couple new options in the menu:

- **Delete**: Delete the current note.

- **Export**: Export the current note to Google Drive or the file system of your Note 3.

- **Add Tag**: Tag the current note with keywords, which you can then search for in the S Note search. Unfortunately, S Finder does not search through S Note tags.

- **Edit Index**: Index the note in the same manner described previously.

- **Print**: Select and print one or more pages using mobile print. (See section on <u>Printing</u> (p.279) for more information. I suggest using a third-party app called PrinterShare instead of the built-in protocols.)

While in view mode, tap the back button to go to the home screen of S Note:

Tap the "Recent Notes" button to switch to a view that includes only recent notes (and then tap "All Notes" to switch back again). Tap the magnifying glass icon to search your notes, including your tags. Tap the plus icon to create a new note. Swipe left and right to see other notes, and drag any note down to preview its pages. You can also tap the gear icon to view options for the note, or the page icon with a plus sign to create a new page in the note.

TIP: The gear icon here has a feature not found elsewhere in S Note—locking. Use this to password protect a note. Do not assume that locking a note will keep extremely sensitive data safe, however. It is a casual form of protection and not the same as encryption.

Tapping the menu button on the home screen of S Note gives you the following options:

- **Use New Template**: Create a new note using a template other than your default.

- **Sync With Evernote**: Back up your S Note data to your Evernote account.

- **Settings**

  - **Sync Account**: Choose to backup your S Note data to your Samsung account or Evernote account.

  - **Change Default Cover**: Change the default cover style you selected when you first ran S Note.

  - **Change Default Template**: Change the default note template you selected when you first ran S Note.

  - **Add Page**: Choose whether to automatically apply your default template to new pages, to always use a blank template, or to ask every time.

  - **Size Of Inserted Image**: Select how much to scale images that you insert into your notes.

  - **Location Tag**: Tag notes with current GPS data. If you use this option, be careful of who you share your notes with.

  - **Downloads**: Show background images and Idea Sketch figures that you have downloaded from Samsung's servers.

  - **Writing Sound**: Play sound while writing or sketching in a note.

  - **Haptic Feedback**: Vibrate while writing or sketching in a note.

  - **Help**: View various tutorials on using S Note.

Scrapbook

The Scrapbook is a more sophisticated version of Easy Clip. Whereas Easy Clip simply captures the selected area and turns it into an image, Scrapbook smartly saves the content you select and extracts rich information from it when applicable. For example, here I have called up Scrapbooker via Air Command and outlined an advertisement on the eBay homepage:

As you can see, Scrapbooker has nearly trimmed the image and extracted applicable text from the web page. From this dialog box that pops up after using Scrapbooker, you can add a memo, tags, or categorize the content by clicking "My scrapbook." The "X" will discard the content, and the checkmark will save it into Scrapbook.

Opening the Scrapbook app itself will bring you to the home page, which displays all of the content you have saved.

As you can see, I have saved a variety of content; a text message, a YouTube page, web content, some app shortcuts, and so on. Try Scrapbooker in any app; it is a pretty good way to clip content for later use.

⭐ *TIP: At the time of publication, the latest YouTube update from the Google Play Store had broken Scrapbooker functionality, preventing you from saving videos in Scrapbook. There are two ways to get around this problem. First, you can go to Settings → General → Application Manager → Downloaded → YouTube and uninstall updates. However, if you do not want to downgrade, you can also save a Scrapbook entry of a YouTube video by clicking the share button in the YouTube app and sharing via Scrapbook.*

While on the home page of Scrapbook, you can either open individual pieces of content, tap "My scrapbook" to manage categories, or tap the menu button. Menu options in Scrapbook include:

- **Select Item**: Select multiple items to share or delete via the buttons in the upper-right-hand corner of the screen, or export, move, or copy via the menu.

- **Change Layout**: Change how your content is displayed on the home page of Scrapbook.

- **Rename**: Rename the current category.

- **Manage Categories**: Delete existing categories. This option will be grayed out if you only have one category. Note that deleting categories WILL delete all of their content as well. If you wish to delete a category but save its content, you must move all of its content to another category first.

- **Import**: Import .scc files that other Scrapbook users have sent you. (You can export and share any Scrapbook entry by opening it, tapping the share icon in the upper-right-hand corner of the screen, and sharing as an .scc file.)

- **View**: Filter the type of content displayed.

- **Accounts**: Enable or disable Scrapbook synchronization with your Samsung Account, if you have one.

- **Location Tag**: Choose whether to tag your Scrapbook files with GPS data. If you do, be careful with whom you share your Scrapbook content.

- **Help**: View short tutorials on using Scrapbook and Easy Clip.

If you open a piece of content saved in your Scrapbook, you can either share or delete it using the buttons in the upper-right-hand corner of the screen, tag it, or pull up the menu. Menu options for an individual piece of content include:

- **Memo**: Create and attach a memo.

- **Move**: Move the memo to a different category.

- **Copy**: Copy the memo to a different category.

- **Edit**: Edit the content itself.

TIP: So, which is better—Scrapbooker or Easy Clip? The way I see it, the only thing Easy Clip does better than Scrapbooker is crop out custom selections. If you want to save an irregularly shaped image, then use Easy Clip and its horseshoe selection button, and add the content to Scrapbook or your preferred app. For all other purposes, Scrapbooker is generally more powerful.

Screen Write

This feature takes a screenshot of your current screen and then opens the screenshot in an editor that allows you to draw or write on it. To use Screen Write, call up Air Command by hovering the S Pen, single pressing the S Pen button, and tapping Screen Write.

In the screenshot below, I have used Screen Write to take a screenshot of one of my home screens, and begun to play tic-tac-toe on it.

From left to right, the buttons on the Screen Write toolbar include:

- **Close/Open**: Hide or show the toolbar.

- **Pen Settings**: Tap this once to enter free-form handwriting mode, in which you can doodle and sketch freely. Tap this again while it is already selected to choose the type of pen (regular pen, pencil, brush, etc.), color, and thickness. When you have configured a pen type that you really like, you can open this window and tap the icon to the left of the "X" to add it as a preset. From that point forward, you can call up the same pen by clicking on the "Preset" tab in Handwriting Mode.

- **Eraser Settings**: Tap this once to enter eraser mode. Tapping it again reveals two options: thickness and "Erase by stroke." When "Erase by stroke" is selected, the eraser will erase the entirety of any continuous stroke by simply touching it. When it is not selected, the eraser will act more like a normal eraser, removing only the portions of the ink that it overlaps. "Clear all" will erase everything on the current page.

- **Crop**: Tap this once to enter crop mode, in which you can select a part of your screenshot to crop. Tapping it again allows you to choose from lasso or rectangle selection. Lasso selection will let you select freely, and rectangle selection is exactly what it sounds like; you will be restricted to selecting with a rectangular selection area.

- **Undo**: Removes the last stroke entered.

- **Redo**: Replaces the last stroke entered if it has been undone.

- **Share Via**: Share the results of Screen Write via an app of your choice.

- **Cancel**: Close and discard the results of Screen Write.

- **Save**: Confirm and save the results of Screen Write. You can find saved Screen Write files in your Gallery.

TIP: You can also call up Screen Write by holding the S Pen button while continuously pressing the S Pen tip on the screen for 1-2 seconds.

Handwriting Recognition Input Mode

The S Pen can also be used to input text via handwriting mode. This option is available anywhere keyboard input is possible. To enable it, tap and hold the settings button to the right of the "Sym" key on the Samsung keyboard, and tap the T (the second icon from left):

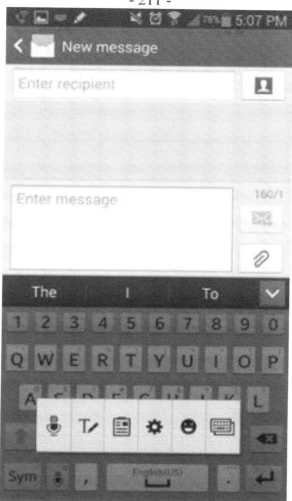

This feature is discussed in more detail in Chapter 5.

Menu And Back Buttons

On the Note 3, you can tap the menu and back buttons using the S Pen. Former Note 2 users will remember that this functionality was missing from the Note 2, which had a complicated gesture system instead. This functionality is very welcome on the Note 3.

Taking Screenshots

As noted in the Screen Write section, you can take screenshots with your S Pen. To do so, hold the S Pen button, and hold the tip against the screen for 1-2 seconds. A screenshot will be taken and opened in an editor. You can make changes if you wish, and then save the screenshot by tapping the checkmark in the upper-right-hand corner of the screen.

TIP: You can also take a screenshot by holding the home button + the power button together for approximately one second.

S Finder

Although S Finder is not an S Pen feature per se, it is closely related to all of the functions I just discussed and is one of the options available in Air Command. S Finder is an app that lets you search the contents of the entire phone all at once. Without S Finder, you would have to open apps individually to search for information—for example, searching for "John" in the phone book would turn up John's contact information, but not any text messages or e-mails in which he participated. S Finder solves this problem by providing a centralized search function for all apps. Notably, S Finder even searches through handwritten content.

S Finder is very minimalistic:

You enter your search term in the search box, and select filters below if you wish (swipe left and right to access more options).

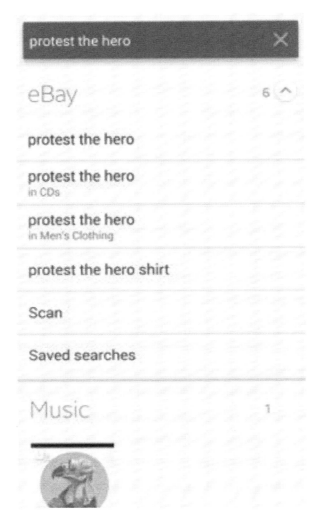

Additionally, you can tap the menu button, then "Settings" and "Select Search Category" to pick which apps S Finder will search.

Although it's very good at finding content on your Note 3, one of S Finder's major limitations is that it cannot search Gmail. Come on, Samsung... you're better than that.

 TIP: In addition to opening S Finder through Air Command, you can open it by holding the menu button for 1-2 seconds.

Automatically Using Handwriting Recognition With The S Pen

It stands to reason that when you have the S Pen out, you want to use it. You can configure the Samsung Keyboard to automatically enter handwriting recognition mode instead of regular keyboard mode when you pull it up with the S Pen detached. Set this up by going to Device Settings → Controls → Language And Input → Gear Icon Next To "Samsung Keyboard" and enable Pen Detection.

S Pen Gesture Guide

If you plan to use the S Pen for handwriting recognition, you should know the correction gestures. You can see them by going to Device Settings → Controls → S Pen → Direct Pen Input → Gesture Guide. They are also provided below, for your convenience.

Chapter 7: Intermediate Functions, Part 2

Congratulations! By now, you should be getting quite comfortable with your Note 3. You've learned how to perform all the basic functions as well as the S Pen features; now we'll start to discuss intermediate-level features and tweaks.

Multitasking With Multi Window

Multi Window allows you to open two apps at the same time, in either portrait or landscape mode:

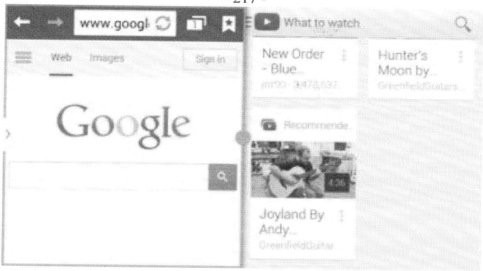

After you have enabled Multi Window, you will see a small icon appear on the edge of your screen. Tapping this icon will pull up the Multi Window control panel, from which you can launch apps to be used in Multi Window mode. You can also tap, hold, and drag this icon to move the control panel.

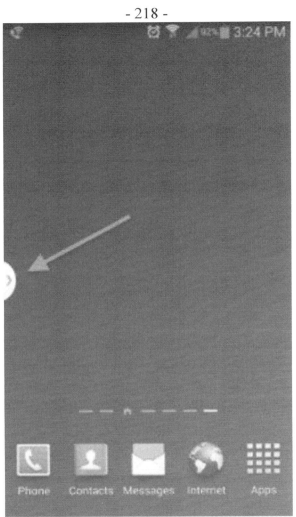

Multi Window is only compatible with certain apps, and not even all the stock apps included on the Note 3. However, there is a third-party app that lets you add any app you want to your Multi Window menu. It requires your Note 3 to be rooted. See the sections on rooting your Note 3 (p.257) and improving Multi Window (p.273).

🏆 *TIP: You can show and hide the Multi Window control panel by holding the back button for about two seconds.*

From the Multi Window settings menu, you can also toggle the setting "Open in multi window view." When this option is selected, the Note 3 will default to a Multi Window view when you open files from within the My Files file manager or the Video app, as well as email attachments in the Email app and text message attachments in the Messages app. This feature does not work in other apps such as Gmail or third-party text messaging apps.

In action, it looks something like this:

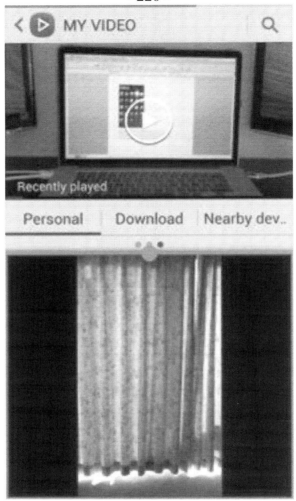

A final feature to note is that you can scroll all the way down the Multi Window toolbar and tap the tiny up arrow to edit the applications shown, or create a new shortcut.

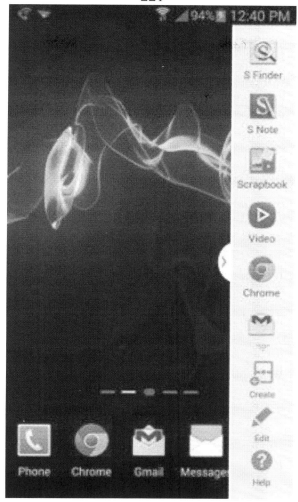

Use the latter option when you already have two screens on the window, and a new *dual* shortcut will be created that opens both of those apps at the same time. For example, here I have created a dual shortcut for Gmail and Chrome:

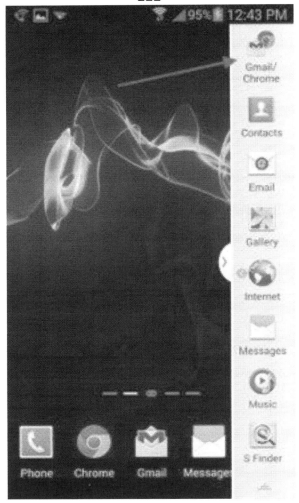

Securing Your Data

Setting Up A Lock Screen

As I noted earlier in this guide, a lock screen is a key data security measure. When enabled, your Note 3 will lock itself after a specified duration while asleep. In this way, if you lose your Note 3, no one will be able to use it or access your data without the unlock code.

To set up a lock screen, go to Device Settings → Device → Lock Screen. There are multiple locking methods available, including:

- **Swipe**: This is a zero-security option that is only useful for preventing the device from being accidentally operated in one's pocket (although if the screen were receiving random input, it would not be hard to accidentally dismiss the lock screen as well). Additionally, a swipe lock screen is the only type of lock screen that allows widgets. Regardless, I strongly suggest you avoid the swipe setting. Most users keep a great deal of sensitive information on their Android smartphones, and if you do not have some type of security measures in place, you will open yourself up to identity theft and other crimes should you lose your Note 3. Using a lock screen with a PIN, password, or other feature is worth the minor inconvenience of having to enter it when you power on your Note 3.

- **Signature**: This lock screen option allows you to unlock your Note 3 by signing your name on the lock screen with the S Pen (with a PIN backup). In general, I do not recommend using signature unlock; although the recognition worked well for me, it is too easy to defeat for someone who has a copy of your signature. I also experienced some problems with the signature lock screen crashing and taking several seconds to correct itself.

- **Pattern**: This unlock option allows you to unlock your Note 3 by drawing a pattern on a 3x3 grid (with a PIN backup). Pattern unlock is more secure than signature unlock, but I still suggest a PIN or password instead. It is often possible to defeat pattern security simply by retracing smudges on the screen.

- **PIN**: This unlock option secures your lock screen with a minimum 4-digit numerical PIN code. There is no maximum PIN length. PIN security is my preferred method of security, as I believe it strikes the right balance between security and convenience. A PIN is much faster and easier to type than a password on a keyboard, and is easier to enter while holding the Note 3 in one hand. I use a six digit PIN.

- **Password**: A password works almost exactly like a PIN, but can include letters and special characters in addition to numbers. A password is more secure than a PIN code in theory, but in my opinion a PIN code is sufficient to deter all but the most determined thieves. The vast majority of thieves are only identity theft opportunists, and care more about selling the device than accessing your information. As long as you make it sufficiently difficult, which I believe a PIN does, you'll be fine.

- **None**: The final option in this menu is to use no lock screen whatsoever. Although this setting is convenient, I suggest carefully thinking through the consequences of losing your phone before using it.

In addition to choosing a locking method, I suggest putting a "Reward If Found" message in the "Owner Information" field, with a phone number to call. This information will be displayed prominently on your lock screen. Also, choose the locking delay and whether to lock instantly with the power key. Personally, I set a 5 second delay without power key locking. That way, if I accidentally hit the power button, I can turn my Note 3 on again without having to enter my PIN.

Encrypting Your Note 3

If you have extremely sensitive data on your Note 3 (for example, so sensitive that attackers would be willing to extract the memory chip to bypass your lock screen), consider encrypting your Note 3. To do so, go to Device Settings → General → Security. Encrypt both the device and your external SD card. This process may take 1-2 hours, so make sure to plug in your Note 3 first.

Locating, Locking, and Remotely Wiping Your Note 3

Google offers a convenient but often overlooked remote locate/erase service. To use these features, you'll need to first ensure your location services are turned on in Device Settings → Connections → Location Services. Enable the "Access to my location" checkbox and at least one location source.

To locate your Note 3, go to https://play.google.com/store on your desktop PC, click the gear icon in the upper-right-hand corner of the screen, and click "Android Device Manager."

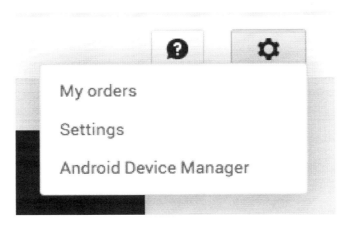

Google will automatically locate your Note 3 if possible, and report its location within a few seconds.

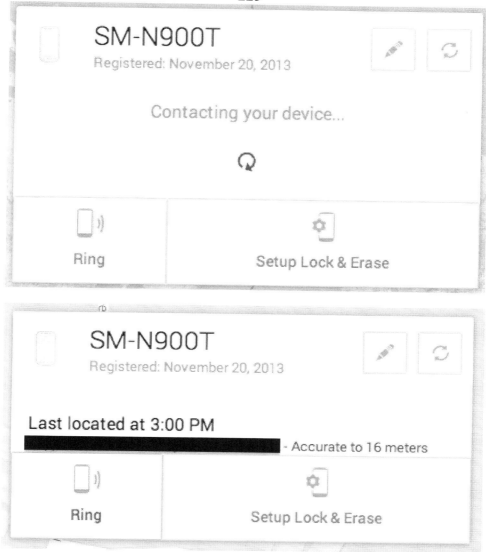

As you can see, Google can locate your Note 3 very precisely using a combination of GPS, cellular, and Wi-Fi signals. Tap "Ring" to have the Note 3 ring at full volume for 5 minutes to help you find your Note 3.

In the unfortunate event that your Note 3 is stolen and not simply lost, you may want to remotely lock and/or wipe the device. Note that you must set up this functionality ahead of time, or you'll be out of luck when you need it.

To initiate setup, first locate your Note 3 as described above, and then click "Setup Lock & Erase." You will be prompted to send a notification to your Note 3, which will pop up in the notification panel.

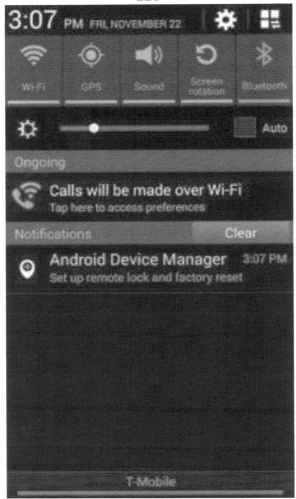

Tap the notification and you'll be prompted to activate the feature. Do so.

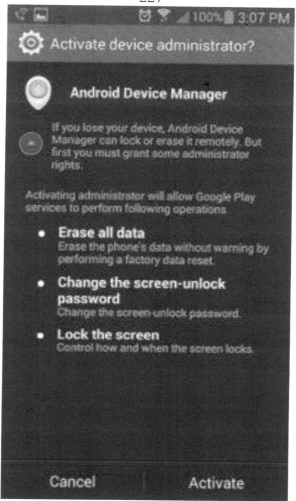

After tapping "Activate," you'll be taken to this settings screen:

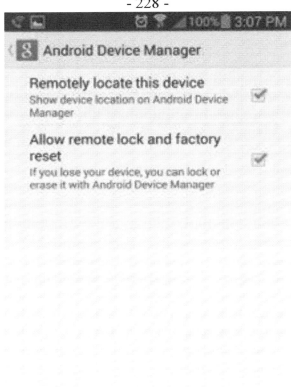

Leave both boxes checked and tap the back button to save your settings. From now on, when you access the Android Device Manager using your desktop PC, you will see these options:

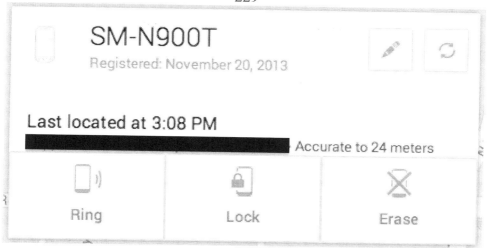

Use them wisely!

⭐ *TIP: If you lose your Note 3 and you haven't set up this feature in advance, you're in trouble. There is a popular app called Plan B that is designed to be installed remotely in this situation, but it is incompatible with the Note 3.*

Attaching Any File You Want To A Gmail Message

For some reason, Google only allows you to attach photos or videos to Gmail messages—at least from inside the Gmail app. A file browser like ES File Explorer, discussed in Chapter 10, allows you to bypass this limitation. To attach any file to a Gmail message, open ES File Explorer and tap and hold to select the file you wish to attach. Tap "More."

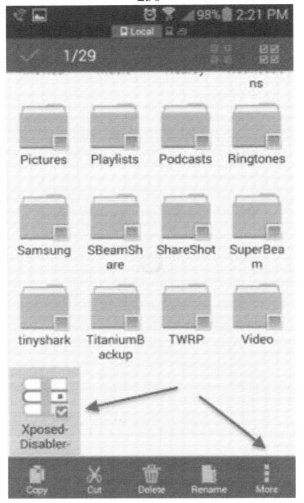

Next, tap "Share" and share via Gmail.

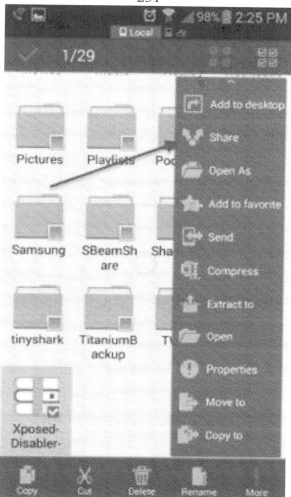

You will then see a new Gmail message, with your file attached.

S Beam, Android Beam, Wi-Fi Direct, DLNA, NFC, WTF?!?

The Note 3 includes a huge variety of wireless features, and it can be very hard to disentangle them. Each of these protocols is something slightly different, so what exactly does each one do?

Let's start with NFC. NFC stands for "Near-Field Communications," and is a fairly new feature in Android smartphones. NFC is essentially synonymous with RFID technology. Sorry to introduce yet another acronym!

RFID tags are tiny chips that can store information, but do not require batteries. They are frequently used for inventory tracking in stores, subway passes, and in swipeless debit and credit cards. In fact, previous Android devices such as the HTC

EVO 4G LTE have supported payments through NFC using an app called Google Wallet. Unfortunately, this feature is missing from the Note 3.

So if not for payments, how does the Note 3 actually use its NFC chip? The first way is through the protocol called "Android Beam," found under the NFC menu in Device Settings → Connections. It is used for sending links, images, contacts, and other content to and from other Android devices that have Android Beam. Data transfer is not actually accomplished through NFC, though—rather, the NFC chips 'handshake' with each other, establishing a *Bluetooth* connection between the two devices that both have Android Beam.

In general, you can expect Android Beam to work with stock apps such as the Gallery, Internet, Contacts, and Music. To use it, open the song/contact/photo/etc. you wish to share, and place both devices back-to-back. When prompted, tap the content you wish to share and then pull the devices apart to initiate data transfer.

The other way that the Note 3 uses NFC technology is to read and write NFC tags, which can automate software actions in conjunction with the Samsung TecTiles app. Read more here (p.273).

So now you understand the relationship between NFC and Android Beam. What about S Beam? S Beam is a Samsung-only feature that sounds quite similar to Android Beam, and in fact, it does exactly the same thing as Android Beam. But whereas Android Beam uses NFC to 'handshake' for a *Bluetooth* connection, S Beam 'handshakes' to establish a *Wi-Fi Direct* connection to send files much faster.

To send files with S Beam, make sure it is turned on for both devices in Device Settings → Connections, and then follow the exact same steps described above for Android Beam.

To summarize, S Beam is a strictly better version of Android Beam, but it's limited because it only works with other recent Samsung devices.

OK, so if S Beam uses NFC to create a Wi-Fi Direct connection, why is there a separate Wi-Fi Direct button in the Wi-Fi settings (Device Menu → Connections → Wi-Fi)? This button lets you directly pair two devices that support Wi-Fi Direct, whether they are Samsung devices or not. You lose the convenience of the automatic NFC handshake, but you gain the ability to transfer data to any Android phone with Wi-Fi Direct. Additionally, with Wi-Fi Direct you can send any file you want using My Files, ES File Explorer, or another file browser, which is not true of S Beam.

To use this feature, open both devices to their respective Wi-Fi Direct settings pages (again, on the Note 3 go to Device Settings → Connections → Wi-Fi → Wi-Fi Direct) and tap on the other device's name under "Available Devices." After successfully pairing the devices, use any app's "Share Via" feature to share a file via Wi-Fi Direct.

However, there is a catch to all of this. There is a third-party program available called SuperBeam (free on the Google Play Store) that is by far the easiest way to establish Wi-Fi Direct connections. It can send any file to any device—Samsung or not—and doesn't even require the devices to have Wi-Fi Direct support in their operating systems. It is an example of how third-party developers can sometimes solve problems better than the OEMs. Read more here (p.304).

I strongly encourage you to use SuperBeam instead of Android Beam, S Beam, or the built-in Wi-Fi Direct feature.

As for DLNA, it is a protocol for streaming videos, photos, and music to and from your Note 3 over Wi-Fi. If you use this feature to share with other Android devices that support DLNA, you will find that your videos, photos, and/or music appear in the other person's Music, and Video apps. Similarly, their media will appear in your apps if they have enabled sharing on their device.

In order for DLNA to function, both devices must be connected to the same Wi-Fi network. Go to Device Settings → Connections → Nearby Devices. Turn this feature on and select the type of content you wish to share. You will then be able to access files on your Note 3 from other DLNA devices. To stream the other direction, open the Music or Video apps and search for nearby devices. Open them, and you'll be able to access their media as well.

Pairing With Bluetooth Devices Such As A Headset Or Car Stereo

Whereas Wi-Fi is used to connect to the Internet through wireless networks, Bluetooth is most commonly used for connecting to car stereos, headsets, keyboards & mice, or other mobile devices. Connecting to a Bluetooth device is usually called "pairing." To pair a device with your Note 3, make sure Bluetooth is turned on in the notification panel, and then go to Device Settings → Connections → Bluetooth.

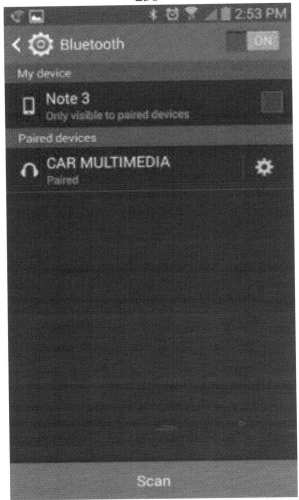

From this screen, tap on your device's name to make it discoverable, which is necessary if you wish to pair it with any other Bluetooth device. Doing so will make it discoverable for only 2 minutes, however, in order to prevent unauthorized devices from attempting to access your Note 3 in the future. You will also need to make the other device discoverable (may be called "pairing mode" or something similar); consult its instruction manual for details.

After you have made both devices discoverable, tap the "Scan" button and wait for the other device to appear under "Available Devices." Once it has, tap on it and follow the prompts to pair the devices. You will probably have to confirm a PIN code on both devices to establish a connection.

In the screenshot below, my Note 3 is paired with my car's stereo and navigation system, entitled "CAR MULTIMEDIA." By clicking the gear icon to the right of the device, you can un-pair the device, rename it, or customize the connection (i.e., for my car I can specify whether to use the Note 3 for call audio, media audio, or both).

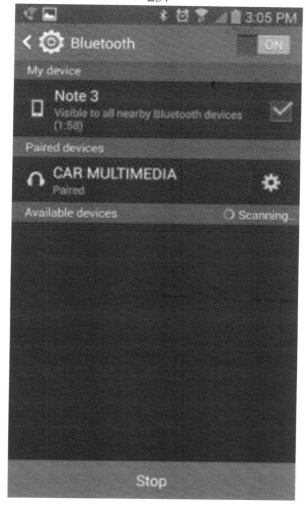

Setting Up A Wi-Fi Hotspot And Tethering Your Computer

The tethering/hot spot feature allows you to share your cellular Internet connection with another device, such as a laptop, a desktop computer, or even another Android device. It makes your Note 3 act as a router.

Note that it may fail to turn on if you do not pay for it; all major U.S. carriers bill wireless hotspots as an add-on that generally runs between $20-30 per month.

To turn on the hotspot, go to Device Settings → Connections → Tethering and Mobile HotSpot. Depending on your carrier, this option may have a slightly different name.

Upon switching the hotspot on, you will be prompted to enter a name (SSID) for your network, select a security protocol (use WPA2 PSK), and specify a password.

You may also see settings that let you hide the SSID, adjust the transmit power, and so on. I strongly suggest you do not change these from their defaults.

After you have created a Wi-Fi network using your wireless hotspot feature, connect to it from your laptop or other device just as you would connect to your home network. If you have trouble connecting, reset your Note 3 by holding the power button and tapping "Restart," and restart the other device as well before trying again.

 *TIP: By rooting your phone, you can enable Wi-Fi tethering without paying extra fees. See **this section** (p.268) for more information.*

Airplane Mode: Obsolete?

As you most likely know, airplane mode disables all wireless connections on your Note 3, including Wi-Fi, Bluetooth, hotspots, and so on. It can come in handy when you want to ensure you are not interrupted, or to prevent your Note 3 from depleting its own battery by searching for a signal in dead zones. But as of October 2013, it's no longer needed when flying.

In October 2013, the Federal Aviation Administration (FAA) announced that airlines are permitted to allow passengers to use electronic devices gate-to-gate. No longer will it be necessary to power off all devices before takeoff and landing. At the time of publication, all major airlines had changed their policies to allow this. So, instead of using Airplane mode the next time you fly, you might want to only disable cellular data in Settings → More Networks → Mobile Networks → Mobile Data. You won't get cell coverage at 30,000 feet, but you'll be able to connect to the plane's Wi-Fi network from the very first minute you sit down!

Preventing Extra Charges By Capping Your Data Usage

If you have a limited amount of bandwidth on your cell plan, you can set a hard limit to ensure your Note 3 doesn't rack up overage charges. To set it, go to Device Settings → Connections → Data Usage and check "Set mobile data limit."

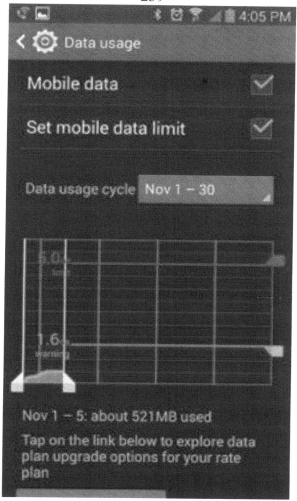

Set the data usage cycle appropriately, and then adjust the red slider up and down to specify the maximum amount of cellular data your Note 3 is allowed to use during that period. As soon as you reach the limit, your Note 3 will shut off cellular data. Of course, you can always return to this screen and uncheck "Set mobile data limit" if you need to.

Mirroring Your Note 3's Screen On Another Display

The Note 3's Screen Mirroring feature allows you to wirelessly share your Note 3's screen on an external TV. Your Note 3 can directly connect to newer Samsung wireless TVs with AllShare support, but if you don't have one—which most people don't—you must purchase a physical device from Samsung called the AllShare Cast Hub. At the time of publication, this device cost $99.99 from Samsung but was available at a substantial discount from third-party retailers such as Amazon.

Screen mirroring is useful for tasks such as streaming video, or displaying photo galleries to an audience.

To use screen mirroring, go to Device Settings → Connections → Screen Mirroring. Ensure that the slider switch in the upper-right-hand corner of the screen is set to "On." You may need to put your TV or AllShare Cast Hub in sharing mode—consult their instruction manuals if you are unsure. Once your Samsung TV of AllShare Cast Hub is prepared, your Note 3 will automatically detect it. If it does not connect automatically, tap the device it detected and follow any required prompts.

*TIP: It is also possible to share your screen via a wired connection, using Samsung's MHL 2.0 HDTV Smart Adapter (MSRP $39.99; **http://www.samsung.com/us/mobile/cell-phones-accessories/ET-H10FAUWESTA**). This option may be easier and cheaper for some users, although it is more cumbersome than a wireless solution. It may be suitable if you are on a budget, and are mostly interested in streaming longer videos and movies during which you will not be holding or operating your Note 3. I recommend purchasing the official Samsung adapter, but if you want a cheaper third-party version, any adapter labeled for the Galaxy S3 or Note 2 will work with your Note 3.*

Disable Annoying Sounds And Vibrations

By default, the Note 3's interface makes a lot of blips and bloops. For those of us who relish peace and quiet, it is easy to disable them. Go to Device Settings → Device → Sound. Uncheck some or all of the following:

- Dialing Keypad Tone

- Touch Sounds

- Screen Lock Sound

- Haptic Feedback

- Key-Tap Sound

- Key-Tap Vibration

Set the Pen Attach/Detach Sound to "Off." I personally do use a notification sound, and I suggest "Beep Once" for professional and non-intrusive notifications.

Giving Your Eyes A Break With Reading Mode

Reading Mode first appeared on the Samsung Galaxy Note 8.0 tablet. It improves the reading experience by adjusting the hue of the screen and increasing text sharpness, thus reducing eye fatigue. In addition to switching on Reading Mode using the slider button in Device Settings → Device → Display, you must enter the Reading Mode menu, tap the pencil icon in the upper-right-hand corner of the screen, and check the box for each app with which you want to use Reading Mode.

Customizing The Notification Panel

You can customize the settings displayed in the notification panel by going to Device Settings → Device → Notification Panel. Enable or disable the screen brightness adjustment setting found in the notification panel, and/or rearrange the toggle buttons. To rearrange buttons, simply tap, hold, and drag them. Releasing a toggle button over another toggle button on this screen will cause the two toggle buttons to swap places.

TalkBack Mode For Users Hard Of Seeing Or Hearing

TalkBack is the main accessibility mode of the Note 3 for users who have limited eyesight. Enable it in Device Settings → Device → Accessibility → TalkBack.

When it is enabled, the entire TouchWiz experience changes. To use the device with TalkBack enabled, you drag your finger around the display, and the device selects different elements and speaks a description of them to you. For example, it will highlight buttons, menu items, and so on. Once you have successfully selected a screen element, you double-tap anywhere on the screen to activate it (the same as a single tap under normal circumstances). Scrolling is accomplished by swiping up and down with two fingers at once. Similarly, you pull down the notification panel by using two fingers, although you have to be very deliberate in this action. If you are having trouble, place your fingers close together and firmly swipe down from the top of the screen.

Zooming In On Any Screen

The Note 3 has a very cool zoom feature that allows you to triple tap on *any* screen to zoom in. Enable it in Device Settings → Device → Accessibility → Magnification Gestures. Triple-tap anywhere to zoom in, and then pan using two fingers. You can also triple-tap and hold the third tap to temporarily zoom in.

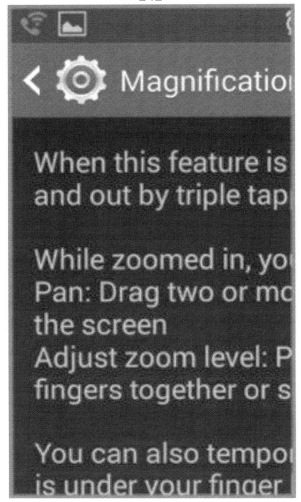

Blocking Unwanted Calls

The Note 3 can block particular phone numbers, numbers containing certain values, and more. To block a contact in your Contacts app, open their details, tap the menu button, and then "Add To Reject List." When you receive a call from a number on your reject list, you won't know it at all.

To manage your reject list or to create a more sophisticated filter (e.g., block all 602 area codes), go to Device Settings → Device → Call → Call Rejection.

Answer Calls Easily With The Home Button

This is a cool feature that makes it easier to answer phone calls that you do want. Go to Device Settings → Device → Call → Answering/Ending Calls and enable "The Home Key Answers Calls." In addition to swiping the green icon to answer incoming calls, you'll be able to simply hit the home button, which can be a lot easier if you're driving or only have one hand free.

Set Up Auto Redial—Goodbye, Dropped Calls

The auto redial option makes dropped and failed calls a little less annoying. With this option enabled, your Note 3 will automatically redial calls that fail to connect, or that drop in mid-conversation. To enable it, go to Device Settings → Device → Call → Additional Settings and enable "Auto Redial."

Configuring Hands-Free Options And Voice Commands

The Note 3 has some hands-free options that are useful if you drive a lot or otherwise aren't available to pick up your Note 3. Go to Device Settings → Controls → Hands-Free Mode to activate various shortcuts.

With the exception of the Air call-accept setting, which allows you to answer calls by waving your hand over the screen, these options all have to do with reading information out loud so you do not have to pick up your Note 3 and look at it. For example, you can have your Note 3 read the names of incoming callers, Calendar alarms, and so on.

Voice commands complement the Note 3's hands-free options nicely, and are available in Device Settings → Controls → Voice Control. You can answer or reject calls by speaking, stop or snooze alarms, and more.

Use S Pen Keeper To Avoid Losing Your S Pen

The S Pen Keeper sounds an alarm if you walk away without your S Pen. Enable it in Device Settings → Controls → S Pen.

Note that this feature only operates when the screen is turned off. Furthermore, it uses the Note 3's pedometer function—that is, it physically senses steps rather than distance between the Note 3 and S Pen. Keep this in mind if you plan to use this feature, as it is still possible to separate the Note 3 and S Pen without triggering the alarm. And of course, if you walk away with your S Pen but not your Note 3 (an unlikely scenario, admittedly), S Pen Keeper won't help you at all.

Configuring One-Handed Operation

Since the Note 3 is such a large device, Samsung has included some features to improve the ease of one-handed use. Depending on the size of your hands and how you hold the Note 3, you may or may not find these options useful.

Enable one-handed operation in Device Settings → Controls → One-Handed Operation. Available settings include:

- **Use For All Screens**: Enable a feature wherein you can quickly reduce the size of the screen to improve one-handed operation. With this option enabled, on any screen quickly swipe from either the left or right edge, to the center, and then back to the edge. Your screen will shrink as shown below. The left icon at the upper-right-hand corner of the shrunken screen allows you to move and resize the screen. The right icon returns your Note 3 to normal operation.

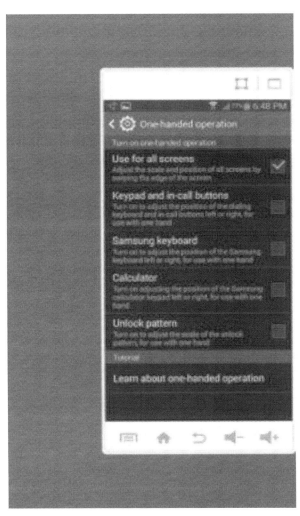

- **Keypad And In-Call Buttons**: Decreases the size of the on-screen dialing keypad and moves it to one side of the screen for easier one-handed operation. Tap the arrow next to the dialing keypad to move it to the opposite side of the screen.

- **Samsung Keyboard**: Decreases the size of the Samsung keyboard and moves it to one side in the same fashion as the dialing keypad shown above.

See Helpful Information By Hovering Your Finger—Wait, What?

Air View is a very cool feature of the Note 3—perhaps the coolest. It allows you to hover your S Pen *or* finger above certain screen elements to pop up additional information. That's right—the Note 3 can detect your finger even when you don't touch the screen. It does so using a technology from Synaptics called ClearPad®.

Read more about this feature in Chapter 6.

Configuring Motions

The Note 3 supports some genuinely useful motion controls. For example, you can automatically call the contact on-screen by raising the Note 3 to your ear, or silence it by placing it facedown on a surface. To enable these and other motions, go to Device Settings → Controls → Motions.

Configuring Smart Screen Features

The Note 3 has several experimental features that use the front camera to observe your face and perform actions accordingly. I think these features are curiosities more than anything else, but they are still interesting to try out, and may be a sign of things to come in future devices.

To enable Smart Screen features, go to Device Settings → Controls → Smart Screen. Available options include:

- **Smart Stay**: Keeps the screen on as long as you are looking at it, regardless of the screen timeout setting.

- **Smart Rotation**: Rotates the screen according to the orientation of your face, overriding the default gravity sensor. Useful if you want to use the Note 3 while lying on your side, as without Smart Rotation, the orientation will be wrong.

- **Smart Pause**: Pause video when you look away from the screen. Works in Video and YouTube apps.

- **Smart Scroll**: Detect your head movement to scroll web pages and lists automatically. Works only in Internet and Email apps.

Enabling Glove Mode For Winter Months

It is possible to increase the sensitivity of the Note 3's screen in order to use it with gloves—and it works with very thick ones. To do so, go to Device Settings → Controls and enable "Increase Touch Sensitivity." If you leave this enabled when you don't need it, you will probably suffer from all kinds of unintended input, so make sure to turn it off when you're done.

Make Your Note 3 Like New With A Factory Reset

Sometimes you need to wipe your Note 3 completely—whether to sell it, or because it's gotten all buggy and you want a fresh start. To factory reset your Note 3, go to Device Settings → General → Backup And Reset. Be warned that this will erase everything on your internal storage, permanently. Make sure you've backed up all the files you need, or at least copied them to your SD card. And on that note, be aware that a factory reset will not affect an external SD card. If you wish to format your SD card, read on to the next tip.

Formatting Your SD Card

To format your SD card, go to Device Settings → General → Storage → Format SD Card. This will permanently wipe all data, so be cautious. It's a good idea to do this when you get a new memory card, to make sure that its file system is completely compatible with your Note 3.

Powering Up Your Ringer While In Your Pocket

Ever have problems hearing your phone ring in your pocket? The Note 3 solves this problem in style by offering a super-loud ringtone when it's in your pocket. It accomplishes this by using the proximity sensor. To enable this super ringtone, go to Device Settings → Device → Call and enable "Increase Volume In Pocket."

Never Miss A Notification With Smart Alert

How often do you pick up your Note 3 throughout the day to check the LED light for notifications? If you're like me, you probably do it all the time. The Note 3 has a special feature where it will vibrate upon being picked up if there are new notifications. This helps ensure you don't miss any notifications as you check throughout the day. To turn these on, go to Device Settings → Controls → Motions → Smart Alert.

Use The Camera Flash For Notifications

The iPhone has offered flash notifications for a while, and Android is only starting to get up to speed. Fortunately, this option is available on the Note 3—a powered-up version of the notification blinker that you can't miss… as long as your Note 3 is upside down! To enable this feature, go to Device Settings → Device → Accessibility and enable "Flash Notification."

Chapter 8: Advanced Functions

By now, we've discussed nearly everything there is to discuss about the Note 3, at least as it comes in the box. In this chapter, you'll learn how to extend the functionality of your Note 3, and take steps toward becoming a power user yourself.

Connecting To Your PC

Installing USB Drivers

Some Android devices support USB Mass Storage Mode out of the box, meaning that computers will automatically mount them as flash drives when connected over USB. Unfortunately, the Note 3 is not one of these devices. If you connect your Note 3 to your PC via USB without the proper drivers, you will only see a lot of failure dialogs. To remedy this situation on Windows, you need to download Samsung's drivers (http://www.samsung.com/us/support/owners/product/SM-N900PZKESPR). Click the link, click the "Downloads" tab, scroll down to the .EXE file download, and download and install the package on your computer. Don't worry if you have a carrier other than Sprint—the USB drivers are the same.

On Mac OS, you don't need any Samsung-specific drivers, but you do need the official Android File Transfer tool (http://www.android.com/filetransfer/).

Accessing Files

On Windows, once you have properly installed the Samsung USB drivers, you can open your Note 3 as you would any other drive. If AutoPlay opens, click "Open device to view files."

If AutoPlay does not open, open Windows Explorer and go to Computer → Note 3.

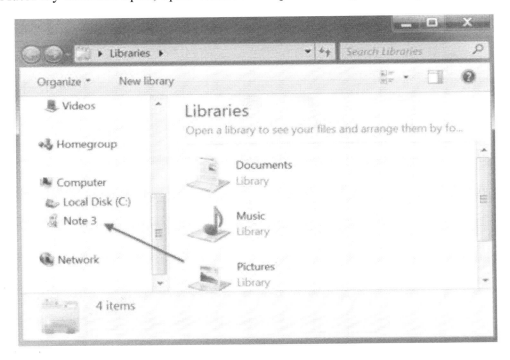

Once you have opened "Note 3," you can open "Phone" to view your Note 3's internal storage, or "Card" to view the contents of its SD card. You can copy, paste, and move files just as you would anywhere else on your PC.

⭐ *TIP: Be very careful about deleting or moving system or app files — only do so if you have a specific reason to.*

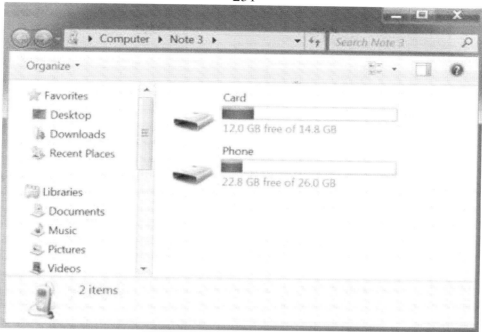

On Mac OS, Android File Transfer will open as soon as you plug in your Note 3's USB cable. Click "Phone" and "Card" to view internal and SD storage, respectively. You can drag files in and out of this window as if it were a Finder window.

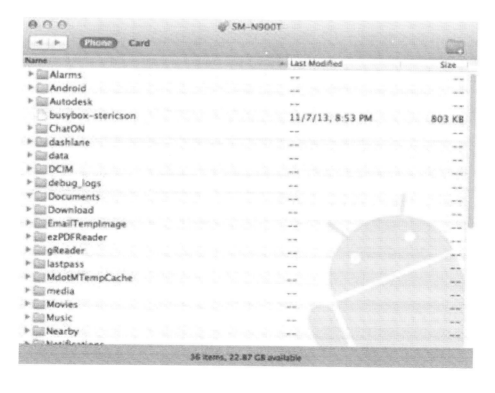

⭐ *TIP: For the fastest file transfer speeds, you will need to enable USB 3.0 manually. To do so, open the notification panel while your Note 3 is connected to your USB 3.0-compatible computer. Tap "Connected as a media device" and enable USB 3.0. Unfortunately, this option may not be available on Mac OSX computers.*

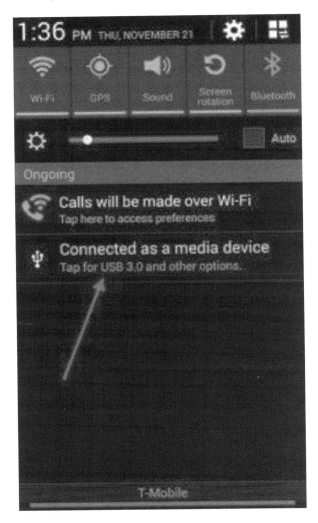

⭐ *TIP: If your Note 3 is having trouble connecting to your computer via USB, make sure USB debugging is switched off in Device Settings → General → Developer Options.*

Samsung Kies

In addition to managing your Note 3's file system, you can also take advantage of backup and media management tools in Samsung Kies, Samsung's synchronization software. It is available for both Windows and Mac OS. I cover only the Windows version below, because the Mac OS version is identical.

Download the appropriate version of Kies from this link (version 3.0 or greater), and install it on your machine. http://www.samsung.com/us/kies/

Kies is pretty straightforward and intuitive. It does two things: backup/restore, and management of your photos, music, video, etc.

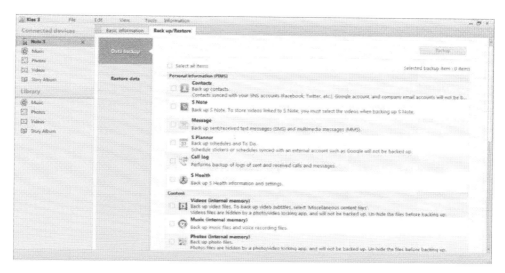

It's a good idea to regularly backup your Note 3 with Kies, although it's generally not necessary to backup every single type of data you can. For example, all of your Contacts should be consolidated in your Google account, so there should be no need to back them up with Kies. However, the ability to backup other data like apps and text messages can be very useful.

Kies Air

Kies Air is a different kind of connectivity program. Whereas Kies is a Windows/Mac program that offers backup and media management, Kies Air is an Android app that offers *only* media management, and does so over Wi-Fi rather than USB. It requires no software to be installed on your desktop computer.

TIP: AirDroid is a popular program that does the same thing as Kies Air, but better. It is more stable and is better designed. Skip to the next section if you want to use AirDroid instead (I recommend it), but if you want to use the official Samsung solution instead, read on.

Get Kies Air from the Play Store app on your Note 3. Install it, and make sure your Note 3 is connected to the same Wi-Fi network as your PC. Your Note 3 will guide you through the setup process.

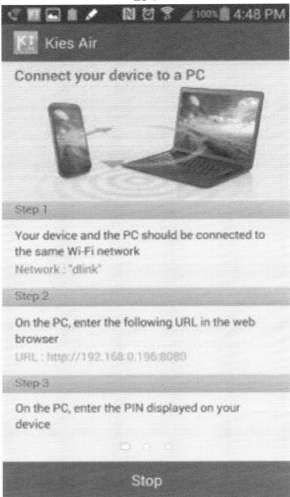

You will be prompted to enter a URL in your PC's web browser, and confirm a PIN code on both devices.

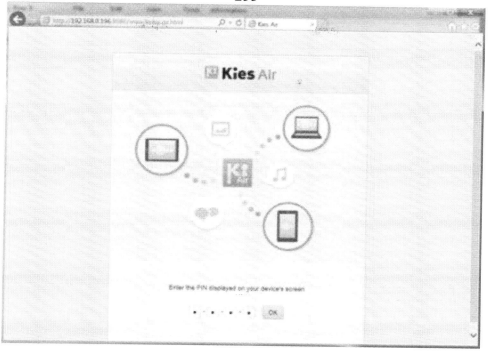

When successfully connected, your Note 3 will display the following screen:

Once connected, you will be able to manage your Note 3 from your web browser. You can view and manage photos, videos, music, ringtones, bookmarks, text message, call logs, contacts, calendar events, and files. Unlike standard Kies, it is missing backup/restore functionality.

AirDroid

As I mentioned above, AirDroid is a free third-party app that does nearly the same thing as Kies Air, but is more streamlined and better regarded by the Android community. Moreover, it can be used with non-Samsung devices, which is advantageous if you ever switch to another brand of phone. I suggest using it instead of Kies Air.

Get AirDroid from the Play Store app on your Note 3. Install it, and make sure your Note 3 is connected to the same Wi-Fi network as your PC. Your Note 3 will guide you through the setup process. You can create an account with AirDroid if you wish, which will give you access to additional features such as Find Phone, but it is not necessary. Also, it is possible to pair your Note 3 with your PC by scanning a QR code instead of entering a PIN, which is a nice feature.

Some of my favorite things to do with AirDroid include reading and sending text messages from my PC browser, and transferring files to my Note 3 over Wi-Fi. I suggest you experiment with it to figure out how it can be useful to you.

Rooting Your Note 3

If you've spent any time on Android discussion forums, you've probably seen people talking about "rooting" their phones. What does this mean, and why would you want to do it?

As you may know, Android is based on Linux, and in Linux (and all Unix-based systems) the most privileged administrator account is called the "root" account. With root privileges, it is possible to execute any code you wish—code that is not normally possible to run.

Here are some things you can do after rooting your Note 3:

- Block all advertisements in browsers *and* apps

- Share your cellular connection over Wi-Fi even if you don't pay for your carrier's hot spot option

- Backup your phone with Titanium Backup and cut Samsung Kies out of the picture

- Install custom ROMs

- Permanently delete bloatware

- … and much more.

In this section, I will show you how to do all of these things.

KNOX Warning

Before we get to the good stuff, I want to give you a word of warning. Remember KNOX, the enterprise security layer built into the Note 3? One downside of this feature is that its heavy-duty security measures get in the way of some things that are easy on the Note 2 and other phones.

On many Android phones, a big draw of rooting is the possibility of installing custom recoveries and ROMs. (A custom ROM is a version of the operating system that has been modified by enthusiasts to include new themes, new features such as call recording, specialized software, and so on. A custom recovery, in short, is software that is necessary to install a custom ROM.)

Unfortunately, the Note 3 has something called a KNOX security flag, which is permanently tripped if you install a custom recovery or ROM. Once the KNOX security flag is tripped, the Note 3 will no longer run the KNOX environment and its warranty is voided. At the time of publication, no developers in the enthusiast community have determined a way to reset the KNOX flag, although it has been confirmed that the flag is theoretically resettable. Still, anyone choosing to install a custom ROM on their Note 3 at this time is likely decreasing the resale value of their phone and eliminating the possibility of ever getting warranty service. I have chosen *not* to install a custom ROM until a KNOX reset procedure is developed.

If you still want to install a custom ROM, continue reading in the next section, "Rooting And Installing A Custom ROM." If, like me, you would prefer to preserve your warranty status and wait until the process is reversible, skip ahead to "Rooting Without Installing A Custom ROM."

Carrier Warnings

At the time of publication, rooting has not come to all carriers equally. As of November 2013, this is the status of each major Note 3 variant:

- **Sprint**: Can only be rooted using CF-Auto-Root, which will trip the KNOX flag.

- **T-Mobile**: Can be rooted using CF-Auto-Root *or* Root de la Vega. The latter will NOT trip the KNOX flag, but it will not permit custom recoveries or ROMs to be installed.

- **Verizon**: Can only be rooted using Root de la Vega, which will not trip the KNOX flag, but will not permit custom recoveries or ROMs to be installed.

- **AT&T**: Same as Verizon.

TIP: There are other rooting packages available, but CF-Auto-Root and Root de la Vega are the most widely tested, and this guide discusses them exclusively.

Rooting And Installing A Custom ROM

WARNING: This procedure will void your warranty and permanently trip your KNOX flag. Furthermore, you must have a Sprint or T-Mobile Note 3; AT&T and Verizon users cannot install custom ROMs at the time of publication.

If you want to root and install a custom ROM, there are really three discrete steps:

1. Root

2. Install a custom recovery

3. Install a custom ROM

To root, you will use software called CF-Auto-Root, and you will need access to a Windows computer and SD card. Go to Settings → General → About Device and write down your model number. It will be something like SM-N900T. Then, follow these instructions precisely:

- MAKE SURE YOU HAVE BACKED UP YOUR DATA. Use Kies if necessary.

- Make sure you have the Samsung USB drivers installed on your computer.

- Download the latest version of ODIN here (get v3.09 or newer) and install it on your computer. http://forum.xda-developers.com/showthread.php?t=2189539

- Go to the CF-Auto-Root homepage and find your device's model number in the first table (entitled "ODIN flashable devices"). http://autoroot.chainfire.eu/

- Click the "File" link to download CF-Auto-Root for your Note 3.

- Extract the .zip file, but do *not* extract the resulting .tar.md5 file.

- Make sure your Note 3 is unplugged from your computer and completely powered down (hold the power key and tap "Power off").

- Hold Volume Down + Home + Power on your Note 3 until it boots into download mode. It may ask you to press Volume Up to continue; do so.

- Start ODIN on your computer (Odin3-vX.X.exe).

- Click the "PDA" button in ODIN and load the .tar.md5 file you extracted earlier.

- Connect your Note 3 and computer via USB. Do not use a USB hub.

- Uncheck the "Repartition" checkbox if it is checked in ODIN.

- Click "Start" and wait for your Note 3 to reboot. Do NOT touch your Note 3 until it has fully rebooted.

That's it—your Note 3 is rooted. If you have trouble, seek help in this thread. http://forum.xda-developers.com/showthread.php?t=2466423

Now, you need to install a custom recovery.

- Open the Google Play Store on your Note 3 and search for "GooManager." Download and install it.

- Open GooManager, tap the menu key, and tap "Install OpenRecoveryScript."

- Follow the dialogs until the Note 3 has fully rebooted.

Now, you've successfully installed TWRP, your custom recovery. This will let you install custom ROMs at will.

To find and install a custom ROM, go to the XDA Sprint Note 3 development forum (http://forum.xda-developers.com/note-3-sprint/development) or the T-Mobile Note 3 development forum (http://forum.xda-developers.com/note-3-tmobile/development). Browse through the various threads tagged [ROM] until you find something that appeals to you.

TIP: You may see odexed and deodexed versions of custom ROMs. I suggest always using the deodexed version; the odexed version can be faster at initial boot, but deodexed ROMs are nearly as fast, and more importantly, are required for many flashable themes and other mods.

If the custom ROM you select has installation instructions, follow them. Otherwise, follow this procedure:

- MAKE SURE YOU HAVE BACKED UP YOUR DATA. Use Kies if necessary.

- Download the custom ROM .zip file. Do NOT unzip it.

- Transfer the .zip file to your SD card.

- Power your Note 3 off completely, and restart it in TWRP recovery mode (hold Volume Up + Home + Power).

- Tap "Wipe."

- Perform a factory reset, then wipe System, Cache, Dalvik Cache, and Internal Storage.

- Go back, and tap "Install."

- Locate the .zip file on your SD card and follow the prompts to install it.

- After installation has completed, tap "Reboot."

That's it! Your Note 3 will restart into your new ROM. Enjoy, and feel free to repeat the process to try out other custom ROMs.

TIP: You can use TWRP to flash a variety of other mods as well, which usually come in .zip format. Read the Other Mods section below for more information.

⭐ *TIP: This method of rooting will not void your warranty status or trip your KNOX flag, but you will be unable to install a custom recovery or ROM. I strongly recommend this option until developers learn how to reset the KNOX flag. This method is available only to T-Mobile, AT&T, and Verizon Note 3 owners. Sprint users can still root their Note 3's, but can only do so using CF-Auto-Root as described in the previous section, which will trip KNOX.*

Even if you do not install a custom ROM, there are still significant benefits to rooting your Note 3, including those mentioned earlier: blocking ads, easy backups, and free Wi-Fi tethering. However, we will use Root de la Vega instead of CF-Auto-Root to avoid tripping the KNOX flag.

- MAKE SURE YOU HAVE BACKED UP YOUR DATA. Use Kies if necessary.

- Make sure you have the Samsung USB drivers installed on your computer.

- Download the latest version of ODIN here (get v3.09 or newer) and install it on your computer. http://forum.xda-developers.com/showthread.php?t=2189539

- Download Root de la Vega from the appropriate source (read the first post carefully for the necessary files; some carriers require only 1 file download, others require 2)

  o T-Mobile: http://forum.xda-developers.com/showthread.php?p=46480545

  o AT&T: http://forum.xda-developers.com/showthread.php?t=2474422

  o Verizon: http://forum.xda-developers.com/showthread.php?t=2481590

- Carefully follow the instructions provided to complete the rooting process.

BusyBox

After rooting your Note 3 with either CF-Auto-Root or Root de la Vega, you will want to install BusyBox, which is a set of utilities required by many root apps.

Open the Google Play Store on your Note 3 and search for "BusyBox." Find the BusyBox app published by Stephen (Stericson) and install it. Open the app, tap "install," and perform a normal (not a smart) installation. Follow the prompts until the installation is complete, and reboot your Note 3.

Blocking Ads With AdAway

One of the best things you can do after you've rooted is to block ads. There are several apps designed for this purpose, but I have found AdAway to be the best. It will block advertisements everywhere on your device—in the stock browser, in Chrome, and in apps.

AdAway is not on the Google Play Store; it is on an alternative platform called F-Droid. Download F-Droid here (https://f-droid.org/) and install it to your Note 3. Search for "AdAway" in F-Droid and install it by tapping the latest version number at the bottom of the screen. Open AdAway, tap the button entitled "Download files and apply ad blocking." Reboot your Note 3 when the process is done, and your Note 3 will be ad-free!

Backing Up With Titanium Backup

Titanium Backup is an Android app that allows you to backup and restore data to an SD card. It accomplishes approximately the same thing as Samsung Kies, but requires neither a PC nor a USB cable, and can be configured to backup your Note 3 on a regular schedule. Moreover, it will work on any non-Samsung phones you purchase in the future. For these reasons, I and many other users prefer to use Titanium Backup instead of Kies.

The free version of Titanium Backup will accomplish basic backups and restores, but purchasing a pro key will give you many more options (~$6.58 on the Google Play Store).

Before using Titanium Backup for the first time, you will need to enable USB debugging. To do so, go to Settings → General → About Device. Double-tap on "Build number" several times and you will get a notification that developer options have been enabled. Go back to General settings, tap "Developer options," switch the slider in the upper-right-hand corner of the screen On, and tick the checkbox next to "USB debugging."

> TIP: In some cases, enabling USB debugging can prevent a proper USB connection with your computer. If you are having trouble connecting over USB, try disabling USB debugging.

To perform a backup with Titanium Backup, open the app and tap the checkmark in the upper-right-hand corner of the screen.

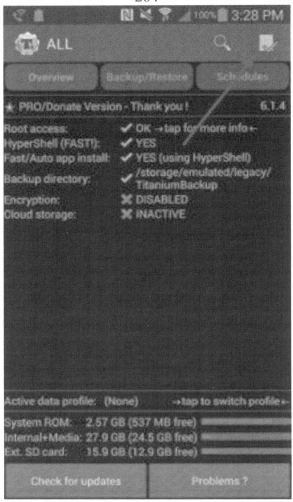

Next, tap the "Run" button next to "Backup all user apps + system data."

Deselect any apps you do not want to backup, and then tap the green checkmark in the upper-right-hand corner of the screen. Your Note 3 will backup all of your apps, app data, and system data to your SD card.

To restore your backup, for example after data loss, tap "Restore missing apps + all system data."

WARNING: It is okay to restore apps and app data when moving to a new custom ROM, but never restore system data on a new custom ROM, or you will cause a multitude of errors and have to start over from scratch.

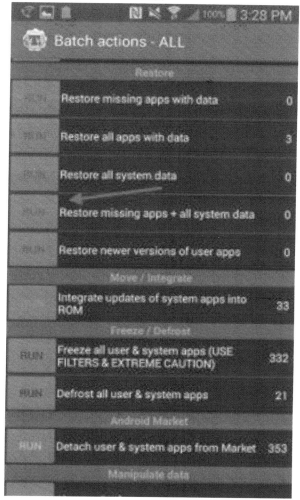

From the next screen, select all of the apps you wish to restore and tap the green checkmark in the upper-right-hand corner of the screen.

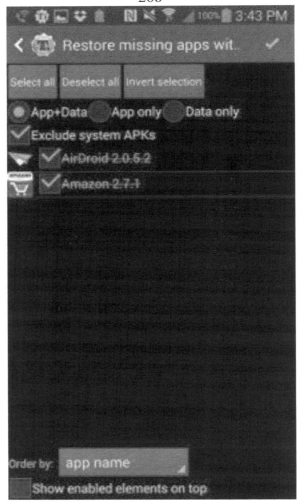

That's all there is to it—unless you want to use any of Titanium Backup's other features, which are numerous. If so, I suggest consulting the official documentation here. http://www.titaniumtrack.com/kb/titanium-backup-kb

TIP: At the time of publication, some Note 3 users were experiencing Force Close problems when restoring backups with Titanium Backup. This issue should be completely fixed in the latest version of Titanium Backup, but if you encounter this problem, seek help in this discussion thread. **http://forum.xda-developers.com/showthread.php?t=2473090**

Tethering With Wi-Fi Tether

Another advantage of rooting is that you can use a Wi-Fi tethering app without paying your carrier's hot spot fees.

WARNING: Although your carrier has no way of knowing with certainty that you are tethering, you will likely set off the alarm bells if you use a massive amount of bandwidth. I advise against using this method to stream video or download massive files. Use it for regular web browsing and you will be fine. Of course, I take no responsibility for your actions if you choose to violate the terms of your agreement!

On the Note 2 and many other recent Android phones, the Wi-Fi tethering app of choice has been Wi-Fi Tether-TrevE Mod. However, its developer has not updated it since April 2013, and the last version does not work with the Note 3.

The best alternative at this time is an app in the Google Play Store called "WiFi Tether Router" ($1.95). Most Note 3 users report it works well, and the developer has a reputation for responsiveness, so the risk is very minimal. It works well for me.

TIP: Do not buy WiFi Tether Router unless you have rooted your Note 3. If you are not rooted, you will waste $1.95 and not be able to use the app.

Removing Bloatware

"Bloatware" is a term for undesirable software that comes pre-installed. Not everyone will necessarily agree on whether a particular pre-loaded app is bloatware, but, for example, most users would probably agree that the TripAdvisor app that comes on the Note 3 is unnecessary. Most users probably have their own preferred travel services.

Without rooting or installing Titanium Backup, you can only "disable" bloatware, and this function is blocked for some apps such as Flipboard. By rooting your Note 3, you can permanently remove these applications using Titanium Backup, freeing up additional memory on your Note 3.

To do so, root your Note 3 and install Titanium Backup as described above. Then, go to the preferences menu of Titanium Backup and make sure "Chuck Norris Mode" is enabled. Ignore the Bloatware Melter option—it's not necessary on the Note 3.

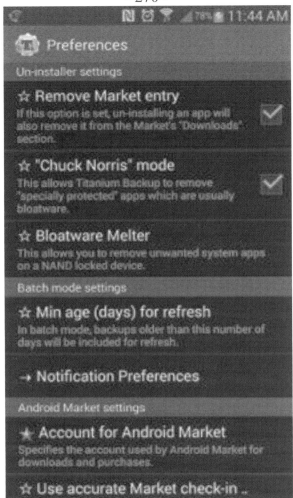

Return to the home screen of Titanium Backup and go to the "Backup/Restore" tab:

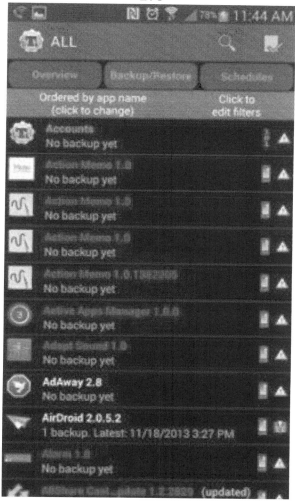

Tap on the package you wish to permanently delete, and you'll see this dialog:

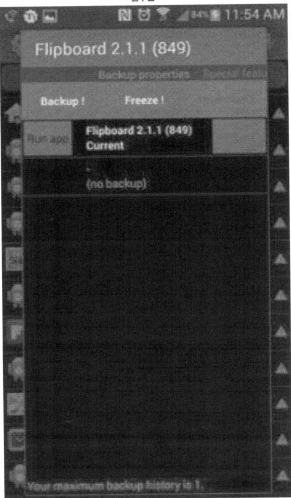

Tap the red "Un-install!" button in the upper-right-hand corner of the screen and approve the confirmation boxes that appear. The Note 3 will permanently delete the application from your ROM.

To make sure you don't delete anything important, consult this spreadsheet. It is maintained by a group of Note 3 users and tells you what packages you can delete without causing errors.
https://docs.google.com/spreadsheet/ccc?key=0AmzC8GFarItSdGpOZzBfWlR4M C03aDMyZ1BDUFNqU0E&usp=sharing#gid=0

WARNING: Deleting packages this way is permanent. They will *never* return, even after a factory reset. The only way to get them back is to re-install your ROM, a process not covered in this book. Only uninstall packages you're 100% sure you'll never need or want again.

Improving Multi Window And Pen Window

On the stock Note 3, Samsung has only enabled certain apps to run in Multi Window and Pen Window. By rooting your Note 3 and installing some third-party apps, you can run any apps you want in Multi Window or Pen Window.

To do this, first root your Note 3 as described above. Second, either or both of the following apps from the Google Play Store:

- MULTIWINDOW Apps Manager

- PEN Window Manager

Open these, select the apps you wish to use in Multi Window or Pen Window, and tap the save (floppy disk) icon at the bottom of the screen. Reboot your Note 3, and the changes will be made. Note that you can also deselect apps that are available by default.

TIP: Although most apps work fine in either Multi Window or Pen Window modes, some may be buggy or cause your menus to slow down. If this happens, you can Google for a specific solution, but you are probably out of luck. However, the vast majority of apps I tested worked fine.

Other Mods

Developers are always hard at work creating new apps and mods for the Note 3. You can peruse XDA's Galaxy Note 3 Themes and Apps section for new root-friendly apps and hacks. http://forum.xda-developers.com/galaxy-note-3/themes-apps

TIP: You cannot use any app or mod that requires flashing a .zip file unless you install a custom recovery. As I discussed earlier, this will trip the KNOX flag and void your warranty. Unless you're willing to take this step, stick to the apps and mods that do not require flashing.

Using NFC Tags

One cool and little-known feature of the Note 3 is its compatibility with Samsung's TecTiles RFID tags. These are tiny 1x1" stickers with embedded RFID tags. You can place them around your home, car, or office, and program them to do different tasks when you tap your Note 3 on them. For example, you might stick one on your car's dashboard, and program it to toggle GPS, open the Maps app, and start playing music.

To use TecTiles, first remove them from their protective sleeve. Tear one off. Make sure NFC is enabled in your Note 3's Connections settings menu. Tap your Note 3 on the TecTile you ripped off and your Note 3 will prompt you to open the TecTile app on the Google Play Store. Install and open it.

The app is fairly intuitive. Tap one of the four buttons to select an action for your TecTile:

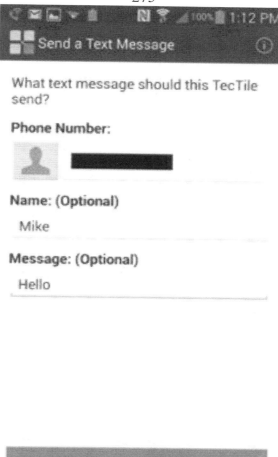

Here, I have instructed the TecTile to send a text message, and entered contact details. After specifying the first action, you will be taken to a new screen where you can review and add additional actions for the TecTile:

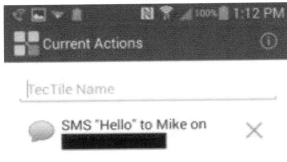

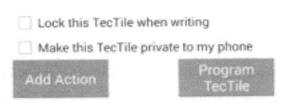

When you have added all the actions you want, tap "Program TecTile" and you'll see this screen:

This TecTile can be read by any NFC equipped phone

Hold Over TecTile To Program

Write multiple TecTiles with the same actions

Hold the back of your Note 3 to the TecTile and it will be programmed.

The other major feature of the TecTile app is its ability to set different Profiles (in the Settings & Apps category). These profiles can be customized in the "Profiles" tab. I have a night and a normal profile, and one NFC tag on the wall next to my bed that switches between them. At night, I tap my Note 3 to decrease the brightness, silence it, and open the Clock app so I can set an alarm. (The TecTile app has a built in alarm clock, but I prefer to use the system app.) In the morning, I tap my Note 3 on the same TecTile to turn up the brightness, and turn my ringer on again.

USB OTG

USB OTG (On-The-Go) is another little-known feature of Android, and is fully supported on the Note 3. Purchase a USB OTG adapter like this one (http://www.amazon.com/eForCity-Adapter-compatible-Samsung%C2%A9-Galaxy/dp/B00871Q5PI), and you'll be able to connect USB flash drives, mice, keyboards, game controllers, and other accessories to your Note 3. It is even possible to use USB OTG in conjunction with a USB hub, to connect multiple devices at the same time.

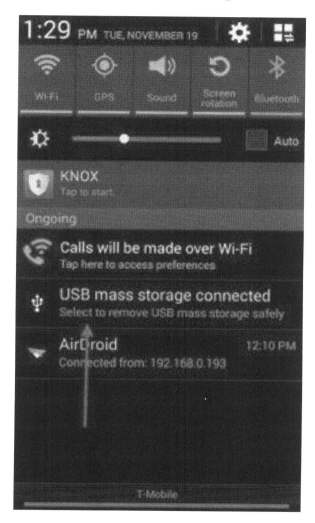

TIP: If connecting a USB drive, you will need to eject it before unplugging the USB OTG cable. To do so, open the notification panel and tap the notification. Wait a few seconds until you see a confirmation message.

Printing

Although the Note 3 has some built-in printing functionality, it is not very well developed and is likely to be more trouble than it's worth. If you need to print from your Note 3, I strongly suggest purchasing PrinterShare Mobile Print from the Google Play Store ($12.95). It is compatible with a wide range of printers, and the free version will let you print test pages to determine if it's worth the investment. If it works with your printer, you will save yourself a big headache by purchasing this app.

Installing Adobe Flash

Although Flash is slowly being phased out in favor of newer technologies like HTML5, it is still common enough that you might want it on your Note 3. Flash is no longer in the Google Play Store, but you can download and install the last archived version directly from Adobe's site: http://download.macromedia.com/pub/flashplayer/installers/archive/android/11.1.1 15.81/install_flash_player_ics.apk

Neither Chrome nor the stock Internet browser support Flash, so you will need to download a third-party alternative. I recommend UC Browser, available free from the Google Play Store.

Saving Battery Power

On Android devices in general, the greatest source of power consumption is the screen. On the Note 3, you will notice a massive difference in battery life depending on the brightness setting you use. If you're having battery life woes, this is the first thing to check. I find that on the Note 3, even 20% brightness is more than enough for comfortable usage, except perhaps in bright sunlight.

TIP: The Note 3 has a Super AMOLED screen, which does not have a backlight—rather, the brightness of each individual pixel is controlled. This means that it takes less power to display darker colors. One trick to further reduce your screen's power consumption is to use dark wallpaper and set apps to use dark themes when possible.

The second greatest source of battery drain is apps themselves. In general, you will notice your battery life decline as you install more apps—and to some degree, this is understandable. If you are installing apps that perform background services, which many do, they will use some power. However, many apps are poorly coded and drain much more than their fair share of battery power. Try to only install reputable apps, (p.159) and if your battery is draining faster than it should, uninstall or disable apps you're not using.

You can view estimates of battery usage by app in Settings → General → Battery. If you are having a serious problem and can't seem to find the culprit, your only option may be to factory reset your Note 3 and install apps a couple at a time until you identify the offender.

Here are some additional ways to steal back battery life:

- Enable power saving mode in Device Settings → General.

- Use Wi-Fi instead of cellular networks when possible; the Wi-Fi radio requires much less power. Some people think that turning Wi-Fi off saves battery life throughout the day. This may be true if your Wi-Fi radio will just be searching, but if you'll be in range of a wireless network, you'll actually save more battery power just by staying connected to it instead of the cell tower.

- Delete unused widgets from your home screens and disable unused features in Device Settings.

- Turn off S Pen Detection in Device Settings → Controls → S Pen.

TIP: Advanced users may want to check out BetterBatteryStats ($2.89 on the Google Play Store). It has a steep learning curve beyond the scope of this book, but is a very powerful tool for determining what is draining your battery.

Keeping Your Battery Healthy

To make your battery last as long as possible over the long run, try to run it down to ~10% every couple weeks—but try not to go much lower, and if you must, charge it up as soon as possible thereafter. It's okay to run it down to 10% more often—just don't let it drain all the way and sit idle for an extended period of time, as that's the best way to ruin your battery. If you treat you battery properly, it should last for as long as you have the Note 3.

TIP: Use the included charger to charge the Note 3 when possible, as it outputs much more current than most smartphones' chargers. However, contrary to some reports on the Internet, it is not necessary to use a USB 3.0 cable to achieve maximum charging speed. A USB 2.0 cable will charge your Note 3 just as quickly, as long as it's connected to the appropriate charger. Note that charging via a computer's USB port will take much longer than with the included charger.

Online Resources / Getting Help With Your Note 3

There are numerous Android-related online communities, but two of my favorites are Android Central and XDA. Android Central is an excellent source of Android news and reviews, while XDA is my preferred source for all things related to rooting and customization. The main Note 3 forum on XDA is located here (http://forum.xda-developers.com/galaxy-note-3), but the site has dedicated forums for each of the major carriers:

- **Sprint**: http://forum.xda-developers.com/note-3-sprint

- **T-Mobile**: http://forum.xda-developers.com/note-3-tmobile

- **Verizon**: http://forum.xda-developers.com/verizon-galaxy-note-3

- **AT&T**: http://forum.xda-developers.com/note-3-att

Either of these websites is a good place to ask for help with your Note 3—but in my experience, XDA is a better place to seek help with more difficult/technical issues.

Chapter 9: What Are These Apps?

Good work. By now, you know more about the Note 3 than 99% of other users—but we're not done yet. In this chapter, I will give you a quick rundown of several stock apps (apps that come with the phone) whose functionality may not be immediately obvious. I tell you what each one does—often it is unclear without experimentation—and give you my commentary on its overall usefulness and potential alternatives. The Note 3 includes some very good and interesting apps, but it also includes some "bloatware," junk apps that Samsung gets paid to include but are not the best options out there. For apps that I discuss at length elsewhere in the book, I link you to the relevant discussion.

Bloomberg+

Bloomberg+ provides news, market data (stocks, futures, currency, etc.), and streaming Bloomberg TV. It is among the most popular finance apps on the Google Play Store.

If you closely follow financial news, Bloomberg+ may be useful for you. Otherwise, you're much better off using a full-featured news app, such as Flipboard or GReader. Such apps can pull news from multiple sources—not just financial news—and is more flexible than Bloomberg+. Also, Bloomberg+ caused significant battery drain for me while running in the background, so keep your eye on your battery level if you choose to use it.

ChatON

ChatON is Samsung's proprietary messaging app. It allows you to message other ChatON users without burning through your SMS limit.

The app itself is not badly designed, and the concept is certainly welcome for users with a limited text messaging plan. The fatal flaw is its user base—your friends probably won't have it. Try more mainstream options such as Kik or WhatsApp from the Google Play Store. These apps do the same thing as ChatON, but it's a lot more likely your friends will have them, too.

Downloads

Downloads is a very minimalistic downloaded file manager that keeps track of files you have downloaded from either the stock browser or Chrome. It allows sorting by date or size.

Unless you are a downloading maniac, you will probably rarely use the Downloads app. When a download completes, you receive a notification and can tap it to open the file, so it's usually not even necessary to open the Downloads app when you first download a file. If you do happen to need to see your download history, you will probably find Downloads completely sufficient for your needs. One thing it cannot do is move, copy, or otherwise manipulate downloaded files—for that, you'll need an app like ES File Explorer.

Dropbox

Dropbox is a cloud storage app that is compatible with multiple platforms including Windows and Mac OS. It allows you to upload and download files to and from a virtual hard disk and synchronize your files across multiple devices.

I am a huge advocate of Dropbox. I use it extensively, and save all of my personal and work files to my Dropbox while using my PC, so that I always have them available on my Note 3. In addition to keeping your files backed up and available on the cloud, Dropbox also saves every single version of your files—so you can revert to previous versions if you lose data. This has been invaluable for me and many other users. What's more is that many carriers offer a free 48GB upgrade for 2 years with the purchase of a Note 3. If your carrier supports this promotion, you will receive the bonus space when you sign into your Dropbox account on your Note 3 for the first time.

Evernote

Evernote is a cross-platform cloud note-taking app, and supports both Windows and MacOS in addition to Android. On the Note 3, it can also be used to back up your S Notes.

I regularly use Evernote and applaud its inclusion on the Note 3. How many of you simply email notes to yourself? Evernote is a much easier and more secure way of keeping your notes organized and synchronized between devices. Plus, Note 3 users on most carriers receive a free year of Evernote premium service.

Flipboard

Flipboard is a content aggregator, combining news and social media feeds to create a personalized 'magazine.'

Flipboard has a very strong following and many users love it. Personally, it never really grew on me and I find its interface to be distracting. When I read news, I just want to get straight to the information, and raw text works the best for me. I use

GReader. Also, Flipboard loses some of its value if you are not a big social media user, since social network integration is a central feature. Flipboard is a love-it-or-hate-it type app, so I suggest you at least give it a try.

Google

If you have enabled Google Now, this will open it. If you have not, it will simply open a Google search utility.

The Google app works fine for what it is, although I have never found a need to use it. When I want to search Google, I simply open Chrome and search. When I want to access Google Now, I hold the home key and tap the "G" button.

See more information about Google Now here (p.164).

Google Settings

Google Settings allows you to customize a few Android-related options in your Google account, right on your Note 3.

It is helpful to be aware of the settings in this app, although you will probably only rarely use it, if ever. If you want to investigate the options available in your Google account, you'll want to use the desktop site instead of this limited app (https://www.google.com/dashboard).

Google+

Google+ is the mobile client for Google's social network alternative to Facebook. It will let you interact with other users (friends, family, etc.) who also use Google+.

If you are among the select group of Google+ enthusiasts, this is the only game in town. If you're new to social networks in general, you'll probably want to look at Facebook before Google+, because it has a much, much larger user base. I have resisted using Google+ because Google has pushed it in ways I don't like, such as trying to force users to use their real names as YouTube screen names through Google+.

Group Play

Group Play allows you to share music, pictures, video, documents, and play games over Wi-Fi with other Samsung smartphone users in close proximity to you.

While Group Play is an interesting concept, it is unlikely you will ever have a reason or opportunity to use it. Even if you found a group of Samsung smartphone users who knew how to use Group Play and wanted to do so, it is honestly easier to share files via email, Dropbox, or just handing over your phone! I see Group Play as an experimental concept—interesting, but very useless.

Hangouts

Hangouts is the mobile client for Google's chat platform—the same one you see when you're logged into Gmail. It replaced Google Talk in 2013.

Hangouts is a fine app and Google has put a lot of effort into improving it since it came out. It does not significantly drain your battery while running and works very well for text or video chatting with your contacts. If you use Gmail chat a lot, Hangouts is the best program for doing so on your Note 3.

KNOX

KNOX is a very interesting security platform. It allows you to run a second, "contained" version of your operating system that is encrypted and totally separate from everything else on your device. Samsung markets it as a way to have a separate work device on your phone without actually carrying two devices, although you can use it for whatever purpose you like. There are some significant downsides; notably, you only have access to the KNOX store, not the Google Play Store.

The majority of users probably will never need or want to use KNOX, but some business users may find it extremely useful. Anyone with a need to keep data (1) secure and (2) separate should try out KNOX.

My Files

My Files is the stock file manager app. It lets you access the file system of your Note 3 and your SD card.

My Files works, but it is inferior and limited compared to the excellent and free ES File Explorer. ES File Explorer has a better interface, allows root access to file directories, and is frequently updated. Ditch My Files and don't look back.

PEN.UP

PEN.UP is a social networking app for sharing S Pen artwork.

Artists and art aficionados should check out PEN.UP to see what kind of art other Note users are creating with their S Pens. If you feel compelled, you can of course submit your own.

Play Books/Games/Magazines/Movies & TV/Music

This is a group of apps that complement the Play Store. They allow you to buy and consume media (movies, music, books, magazines, etc.) from Google.

All of these apps work as advertised. Whether you use them or not will likely depend on the degree to which you've already bought into other ecosystems. For example, I read all of my eBooks on my Kindle, so I buy eBooks exclusively from Amazon, and never from Play Books. Similarly, if you are already invested in iTunes, you might not want to buy music from Google Music.

POLARIS Office 5

POLARIS Office 5 is a Microsoft Office-compatible productivity suite. It includes Word, Excel, and PowerPoint functionality.

There are a lot of Office-compatible suites for Android. POLARIS works well in general and is free—you probably won't need anything more for light or occasional document viewing. If you plan to edit extensively and/or need to edit complex documents, you might need to try other Office apps to find the one that works best for your particular needs. If you feel the need to branch out of POLARIS Office, I really like Kingsoft Office (free). You can also try Google's Quickoffice (free), or OfficeSuite Pro 7 ($14.99 in the Google Play Store and highly rated by critics).

S Health

S Health offers several tools to track and maintain your fitness, including a pedometer, a GPS tracker for running, a food tracker, a weight diary, and more.

S Health worked as advertised for me and is worth a shot for anyone who wants to track their physical activity. It is missing some advanced features found in products like the Fitbit One, such as sleep tracking, but the price is right. This is likely a niche app, but it is worth trying if you think it could help you. Some users have reported battery drain while using S Health, so keep an eye on you battery if you choose to use it.

S Note

S Note is Samsung's free-form note-taking app, designed around the S Pen.

S Note is a powerful app, especially with its new charting and graphing features. Most users will find it satisfactory, although it's not perfect. It's slow, it does not do on-the-fly handwriting recognition, and Evernote synchronization leaves something to be desired (it is not possible to edit S Notes in Evernote after they have been synchronized). If you want an alternative, try Papyrus (free in the Google Play Store; premium features available for purchase) or Lecture Notes (~$4.30 in the Google Play Store).

See more information about using S Note here (p.197).

S Translator

S Translator is a translation app that handles voice or text input and output. In other words, you can speak to it, and it will speak the translation back to you.

I can see S Translator coming in handy while traveling. It has a very large library of stock phrases, which are useful more often than not, but still include some oddities ("I have a big face"). It suffers from the same woes as all electronic translation services, but is better than nothing in a pinch. It was bug-free during my tests, but note that you need an active Internet connection to use it, as all translation is performed in the cloud.

S Voice

S Voice is Samsung's voice command system, and offers many of the same commands as Google Now.

I was extremely surprised at how well S Voice performed during my testing. Although its voice recognition is slower than Google Now's, it was more accurate for me and handled my requests just as well, if not better. For users who do not like the proactive card system of Google Now, S Voice is a solid alternative. My guess is that Google Now has more long term potential because it's backed by the power of Google itself, but for the time being, S Voice is not bad at all. I strongly suggest you give it a spin and see whether it might suit your needs better than Google Now.

Samsung Apps

Samsung Apps is Samsung's proprietary app store—a competitor to the Google Play Store.

I suggest avoiding Samsung Apps completely. Once in a while you can find apps cheaper in Samsung Apps than the Play Store, but the selection of apps is no contest. Additionally, if you buy apps through Samsung Apps, you won't be able to install them on future non-Samsung Androids that you own. Not a great trade-off.

Samsung Hub

Samsung Hub is a portal to buy digital content, including music, video, books, and games, from Samsung.

Again, I suggest avoiding this entirely. Samsung's selection is much more limited than Google's, and this app is basically included to sell to customers who don't know any better. If you want to buy some media, use Google Play or another store (Kindle, iTunes, Nook, etc.) as appropriate; there's really no reason to even think about buying from the Samsung Hub.

Samsung Link

Samsung Link allows you to stream music and video from and to your PC, Samsung TVs, and tablets. You can also easily copy and backup media files. Its goal is to allow you to access your media anywhere, anytime, regardless of where it is stored.

Most users will probably never use Samsung Link, and it is mostly redundant with the DLNA features of the Note 3. To use it, you'll need to own multiple Samsung devices, have a burning need for a media sharing solution, and be willing to use very unusual and proprietary software. My suggestion is to skip Samsung Link entirely and stick to DLNA. If you just want to connect your Note 3 to a TV, try the inexpensive but highly functional MHL 2.0 HDTV Smart Adapter (http://www.samsung.com/us/mobile/cell-phones-accessories/ET-H10FAUWESTA) instead of dealing with this app.

Sketchbook for Galaxy

Sketchbook is a drawing/painting app—sort of like S Note for real artists.

I am no artist, but Sketchbook is a very popular app among artsy types. You'll of course be limited by the screen size, but sometimes limitations drive creativity, and you're not likely to find a better drawing/painting app for the Note 3. It's published by AutoDesk, which has a very good reputation for graphics software.

Story Album

Story Album allows you to create digital photo albums from images stored on your Note 3, and order printed/bound copies.

Story Album is pure bloatware. If you want to create a bound and printed photo album, find a nice custom service online instead of relying on this chintzy app. Come on, Samsung…

Trip Advisor

Trip Advisor allows you to find local attractions, find and book hotels, find and book flights, and more.

Use Trip Advisor if you want—but I suggest you consider your other options, and don't rely on it simply because it comes with the Note 3. To find the best information and deals for travel, it's generally best to research using multiple sources. To find local attractions, try Yelp instead, and for travel try apps such as Orbitz, Expedia, and Priceline.

Voice Search

Voice Search is Google's voice search utility. Not only does it let you search Google using your voice, but it also accepts any and all commands that work in Google Now.

Although Voice Search is basically the same thing as Google Now, Google Now doesn't have its own app shortcut. You can use this or the "Google" app instead.

See more information about Google Now and voice commands here (p.164).

WatchON

WatchON is a universal TV remote control that takes advantage of the Note 3's built in IR blaster.

In my tests, WatchON worked wonderfully with my Panasonic plasma television. There are a few random IR remote control alternatives on the Google Play Store, but WatchON works very well and is free. WatchON adds real value to the Note 3.

YouTube

YouTube allows you to watch YouTube videos on your Note 3.

For the most part, the YouTube app is very well designed and has the same functionality as the desktop version. However, in some cases, certain videos are inexplicably not available on mobile devices. Still, it's the only game in town. If you want to download YouTube videos for later use, try an app such as TubeMate (http://tubemate.net/).

Chapter 10: The 50 All-Time Best Android Apps

Below is a list of my all-time best app recommendations, taken from my book, *The 50 ALL-TIME BEST Android Apps*. (http://www.amazon.com/dp/B00L8ES1L2) Some are free and some are paid. I am in no way affiliated with any of the developers, and I stand to gain nothing from your purchases. My recommendations come from my own experience and research.

1Weather

1Weather is an attractive, functional weather app. It contains all the weather information you need, including hourly, daily, and weekly forecasts. It also offers real-time weather mapping, sunrise/sunset information, and push notifications to keep you informed of changing conditions. Plus, you can easily switch between cities when you travel. In my opinion, no other Android weather app comes close to 1Weather's functionality, style, and simplicity.

Price: Free from the Google Play Store / $1.99 in-app purchase to remove ads

AirDroid

AirDroid offers a unique way to control your Android device—using a web browser on your desktop or laptop computer. After you have installed the app on your Android, you just go to http://web.airdroid.com/ in your browser to open the control panel. From there, you can view photos and videos, change your ringtone, manage contacts, send and receive text messages, listen to music on your Android device, transfer files, take screenshots, and more.

In this way, AirDroid is good for many purposes—mass updates of your phone book with the convenience of a keyboard, showing photos on a big screen, transferring files wirelessly instead of over a USB cable, texting on your computer, and more. Plus, it's totally free!

Price: Free from the Google Play Store

Amazon Appstore

Although most apps on the Amazon Appstore can also be found on the Google Play Store, the Amazon Appstore has some important advantages. First, Amazon offers a free app every day. Sometimes the free apps are excellent—for example, I've gotten several office suites for free over the years. Free games are also common. Second, apps sometimes go on sale on the Amazon Appstore but not on the Google Play Store.

The only catch is that if you install apps from the Amazon Appstore and subsequently uninstall the Amazon Appstore itself, those apps will stop working. Simple solution: don't uninstall the Amazon Appstore. After all, you'll need it to check the free app of the day.

Price: Free from http://www.amazon.com/gp/mas/get/android

Authenticator

Google Authenticator is a two-factor security solution that works with many websites that require a password login, including Gmail, Dropbox, Dashlane, and Evernote.

What is a two-factor security solution?

With Authenticator, anyone who logs into your (Gmail, Dropbox, Dashlane, Evernote, etc.) account will be required to input a code generated by Authenticator in addition to the password. This way, even if someone steals your password, they will not be able to log into your account without also having physical possession of your Android. Authenticator even works when your device has no Internet connection. The biggest downside is that only certain websites and software support it.

Price: Free from the Google Play Store

Barcode Scanner

Barcode Scanner allows you to scan barcodes and QR codes. I use it to comparison shop at the store, to quickly pull up reviews of products, and to scan QR codes in viral advertisements. Barcode Scanner also happens to be required for some features in Authenticator.

Price: Free from the Google Play Store

Boson X

Boson X is one of the few Android games that has stood the test of time for me. It is a unique, arcade-style game with a fantastic soundtrack. It is easy to pick up and play when you only have a few minutes to kill, but deep enough to keep you occupied for hours if you want. Not many games strike this balance as well as Boson X.

Price: $2.99 from the Google Play Store

Call Recorder

Have you ever wanted to record voice calls on your Android phone? Although quite expensive at $9.95, Call Recorder by skvalex is the best call recording app available and is capable of recording to both WAV and MP3. Plus, root access is not required for most phones. But before recording any calls, make sure you're aware of the wiretapping laws in your jurisdiction.

Price: Free trial from http://goo.gl/u690rm / $9.95 to buy on the Google Play Store

Cerberus Anti Theft

Most "Best App" lists say that Lookout is the best Android anti theft app available, but I disagree. Cerberus is my security app of choice. Unlike Lookout and most other phone-locating security apps, Cerberus has absolutely no monthly fee—only a one-time purchase of $4. Better yet, it doesn't slow down your phone, doesn't drain your battery, works reliably, and can even hide itself from the app drawer. Its online control panel is simple and streamlined and works every time. I trust Cerberus more than any other app to help me retrieve my Android smartphone should I ever lose it.

Price: Free trial from the Google Play Store / $4 to buy

Chipotle

No, this is not a joke! For a long time, Chipotle only had an iOS app, and they did a poor job of announcing the Android app when they finally released it in late 2013, so I want to spread the word. The app is well-designed, easy to use, and most importantly, allows you to order online and go straight to the register to pick up your order. No more waiting in line. Oh, yeah. Any app that can save 20-30 minutes of my day is a winner. If you don't eat at Chipotle but you do eat at other quick serve restaurants, see if they have a similar app on the Google Play store that will allow you to skip the line. Many do.

Price: Free from the Google Play Store

Chrome to Phone

Chrome to Phone is an app & browser extension combo that lets you instantly send links and text from your desktop browser to your Android device. You must install both the app on your Android and the Chrome extension on your computer. Once installed, just click the Chrome to Phone button in your browser to send the current tab to Chrome on your mobile device. You can also highlight text on your computer, right click, and select "Chrome to Phone" to copy it to your Android's clipboard. It's a very convenient way to quickly get needed information to your Android device.

Price: Free from the Google Play Store

Cloud Print

Want to wirelessly print from your Android device? Cloud Print is a brand new official Google app that lets you do exactly that. You just install a Chrome extension on your desktop or laptop computer, register your printer with Google Cloud Print, install the Android app, and you're set. No printer drivers or complicated wireless settings needed. The Android app lets you print documents, photos, PDFs, and more. You can also print directly from mobile Chrome.

Price: Free from the Google Play Store

Dashlane

Dashlane is a cross-platform password manager. I use it extensively on my desktop to autofill personal information and credit card numbers, generate random passwords, and store my login info for everything. The Android client is a must-have because it makes all your passwords available on the go. If you are looking for a password manager, I highly recommend Dashlane. The Android client isn't perfect (they're still working on autofill for Android) but the overall experience is excellent. I have tried alternatives such as LastPass, and I always come back to Dashlane for its bug-free functionality and clean interface.

Price: Desktop client is free from https://www.dashlane.com, Android client is free from the Google Play Store; subscription (which is necessary for cloud syncing to Android) is $29.99/year

eBay

eBay's mobile app is free and much better than its slow and buggy mobile website. In the past, the official app was actually inferior to a third-party app called Pocket Auctions, but it's come a long way since then. It supports all major features, including search filters, best offers, PayPal payments, and so on. If you're a regular eBay user, get it now. You'll also want to grab the free PayPal app for additional PayPal features beyond auction payments.

Price: Free from the Google Play Store

ES File Explorer

ES File Explorer is a full-featured file manager. Although Androids do not prominently feature a file and folder storage system like on PCs, these things do exist behind the scenes, and ES File Explorer lets you access them. It is much more powerful than the "My Files" app that comes with most Android devices, and I recommend it wholeheartedly for copying, moving, renaming, and deleting files saved on your internal memory or your external SD card. If you've rooted your device, it can also access read-only system partitions.

Price: Free from the Google Play Store

Evernote

Evernote is a cross-platform cloud note-taking app, and supports both Windows and MacOS in addition to Android. How many of us just email notes to ourselves, or scrawl them on the backs of napkins? Evernote is a much easier and more secure way of keeping notes organized and synchronized between devices. Any note you save into Evernote is automatically backed up in the cloud and copied to your other devices, so you'll never lose data or be without your notes. I use Evernote for shopping lists, journaling, organizing notes for my books, brainstorming, and more. And unless you store a ton of images or audio recordings in your notes, you'll be totally fine with the free service.

Price: Free trial from the Google Play Store; desktop version available at https://evernote.com / Premium service $5 per month

Google Drive

Google Drive is so much more than a simple app. Drive gives you cloud storage space, where you can upload and store files from your computer or mobile device. (And if you weren't already aware, you already have a Drive account if you have a Gmail account. Access it at http://drive.google.com.)

The benefits of using Drive are threefold. First, any files saved on your Drive are backed up. If your computer hard drive crashes or you lose your Android device, any files saved to your Drive will survive. Second, since you can access Drive via your computer or the app on your Android, your files are available no matter where you are. Forget to email yourself a file? No problem—as long as your desktop computer has the Drive software installed and you saved the file to your Drive, you can get it with the Android app. Third, Drive saves every version of every file. Accidentally overwrite your thesis? Just log into the web interface and roll back the file.

Personally, I have the Windows/Mac desktop Drive software and the mobile app, and I save all my work files to my Drive folder. This way, I never lose data and I am never without my data.

In the past, I recommended Dropbox instead of Drive. However, Google now offers significantly more free space than Dropbox (15 GB vs. 2 GB), and its paid plans are significantly cheaper (100 GB for $1.99/month vs. $9.99/month.) If you aren't already using Drive, start today.

Price: Free from the Google Play Store

gReader

gReader is an RSS reader that synchronizes with a Feedly account to bring all your news to your Android device. If you aren't familiar with RSS feeds, here's what you need to know: Most news websites and blogs publish them. RSS feeds are files that syndicate all the posts from their respective websites. When you import them into an RSS reader like Feedly, they let you read news from multiple sources all in one place without visiting many different websites, which is fast and convenient. gReader is simply an app for using your Feedly account on your Android device.

If you want the best-looking RSS app, you might prefer the official Feedly app, Pulse, or Flipboard. But for a functional, no-nonsense RSS reader with plenty of functions like offline reading, gReader is the way to go. There is a free version, but the paid version removes ads and provides extra features like better widgets and voice reading of articles.

Price: Free trial from the Google Play Store / $4.69 to buy

GTasks

Many Android devices do not come with a good to-do app, and where those apps do exist, they generally don't sync with Google Tasks. GTasks is a simple to-do list that solves this problem. If you want a simple to-do list that you can access from both your Android and your Gmail account on your computer, GTasks is the way to go. It has a nice, simple interface, and it has never failed to save and synchronize my tasks.

Price: Free trial from the Google Play Store / $4.99 to buy

Key Ring Reward Cards & Coupon

Key Ring stores all of your loyalty and shopping rewards cards. Don't let those frequent flyer miles go to waste! Better yet, it allows you to easily share cards with other Key Ring users and access weekly fliers and coupons that cashiers can scan right from your phone's screen. The one downside is the in-app ads, and there is no premium version to remove them.

Price: Free from the Google Play Store

Kitchen Timer

Kitchen Timer corrects the one-timer-at-a-time deficiency found in most stock Clock apps. Kitchen Timer allows you to set up to three timers at once and doesn't require any unusual installation privileges. It's a great, bare-bones app and is completely free. I use it all the time when I'm cooking two dishes at once.

Price: Free from the Google Play Store

MX Player

MX Player is my favorite video player. Your Android's built-in Video app is probably sufficient if you only watch short clips, but if you watch a lot of movies, TV shows, or files in obscure formats, MX Player will provide a much better experience. It also handles subtitles like a champ. The paid version removes ads.

Price: Free trial from the Google Play Store / CA~$6.00 to buy

Mycelium Bitcoin Wallet

If you don't know what Bitcoin is, you can skip this app. If you do, all you need to know is that Mycelium is the best Bitcoin wallet for Android. It has features that other apps don't, such as full BIP38 paper wallet support, and it's open source so you can be confident it's safe to use. I always keep some bitcoin in my Mycelium wallet in case I stumble upon a store or restaurant that accepts it.

Price: Free from the Google Play Store

Netflix

If you have a Netflix subscription, the Netflix app is a must-have. If you don't have a Netflix subscription, what are you thinking?!? Netflix is one of the best consumer services in today's economy, period. The value is… amazing. Get a subscription so you can watch amazing video like Breaking Bad, House of Cards, Sherlock, Law & Order, and more.

Price: Free from the Google Play Store (Netflix streaming subscription required)

Nova Launcher

Nova Launcher is a highly customizable home screen replacement. If you're tired of the stock look of your device (Samsung TouchWiz, HTC Sense, etc.), then try Nova Launcher. You can customize the number of rows and columns for the apps displayed on each screen, margins, scroll effects, shadows, your app tray, and much more. You can even hide apps from your app drawer.

Price: Free trial from the Google Play Store / $4.00 to buy

Office Suite 7 Pro

Office Suite 7 Pro is an excellent, feature-packed office suite for Android. It is fast, highly compatible, and has a great user interface. Many users believe it is unquestionably the best Microsoft Office replacement for Android. It's not cheap, but if you wait until a major holiday to buy it, you can sometimes get it on sale for $9.99 or less from Google Play and/or the Amazon Appstore. I especially recommend Office Suite 7 Pro if you're a heavy Microsoft Office user and/or you want the best preservation of your documents' formatting. If you are only a casual Microsoft Office user, take a look at Google's free office suite, Quickoffice, instead.

Price: Free 7-day trial from the Google Play Store / $14.99 to buy

Pandora

Pandora is a music-streaming service. Its library of songs is much smaller than Spotify's and it doesn't let you play specific songs, but it's a great resource for discovering new music similar to what you already like. I don't pull up Pandora when I want to hear a specific song, but rather when I want to hear something new. Pandora is free, but you can only skip 6 songs per hour and you will have to endure ads unless you pay for the premium service. I don't really recommend subscribing, though—your money is much better spent with Spotify. Take what you get from Pandora's free service and run with it.

Price: Free from the Google Play Store / subscription service $4.99 per month

PayPal

If you use PayPal for personal payments or business, the Android app is a must-have. It's much faster and easier than using the full PayPal site on a mobile browser and supports most common functions. (Though, it does not have the ability to create a custom invoice, which I would like to see added.) I use it to square up restaurant checks with friends and family, to make online purchases, and to collect money for my business.

Price: Free from the Google Play Store

Play Music

Although Google Play Music is not the best standalone MP3 player on Android (that title belongs to Poweramp, in my opinion), the other features of the Play

Music ecosystem nevertheless make it the best way to listen to your music collection on the go. Why? Google allows you to upload up to 20,000 of your own songs to the cloud—for free—which are then available to stream from your Android via the Play Music app, from your web browser, or from any public computer. This allows you to have your entire music collection available on-demand through your Android, without requiring any storage space. But don't worry—if you want to download music for offline playback, Play Music makes that easy, too. Overall, Play Music is an amazing and free service, and is the absolute best way to take your music collection with you.

Price: Free from the Google Play Store / Download desktop Music Manager from https://support.google.com/googleplay/answer/1229970?hl=en

Pocket Casts

Pocket Casts is, in my opinion, the best podcast app for Android. It does a magnificent job of managing, filtering, downloading, and playing your podcasts, and can even back up your settings to the cloud. Plus, it's really nice to look at.

Price: $3.99 on the Google Play Store

Quickoffice

Quickoffice is Google's free office suite, and is capable of both editing and creating Word, Excel, and PowerPoint files. It has tight integration with Quickoffice, so it makes it easy to save/backup all your documents to your Google Drive account. If you are a casual Microsoft Office user, Quickoffice will be all you need on your Android. However, if you are a heavy Office user or you need the best possible preservation of your documents' formatting, you might want to take a look at Office Suite 7 Pro instead of Quickoffice.

Price: Free from the Google Play Store

RealCalc

RealCalc has a nicer interface than most stock Calculator apps and offers scientific functions. It also supports RPN mode and allows for a great deal of customization. The paid version adds more features such as fraction conversions, landscape mode, and support for degrees and minutes. It's my preferred Android calculator app.

Price: Free trial from the Google Play Store / $3.49 to buy

Reddit is Fun

If you read Reddit, I highly recommend Reddit is Fun. It's a much better way to browse Reddit than using a mobile browser and has all the features you could possibly want. There are a few other Reddit readers on the Google Play Store, but in my experience Reddit is Fun is the best of them.

Price: Free trial from the Google Play Store / $1.99 to buy

Ringtone Maker

Ringtone Maker does exactly what it sounds like: it allows you to edit MP3s and other audio files to create custom ringtones and easily assign them to contacts on your phone. It is much easier to use Ringtone Maker's all-in-one package than to try to use a separate music editor and figure out how to set the resulting file as a ringtone in OS settings. Ringtone Maker is absolutely free and adds a feature that should be, but rarely is, included by default on Android smartphones.

Price: Free from the Google Play Store

Scanner Radio

This app is awesome. It allows you to live stream police and emergency services radio frequencies to your Android. If you are in close proximity to an emergency response, you often can tune into the local frequencies and find out what's going on first-hand. Sometimes, you can even hear foot chases and other criminal pursuits as they happen.

Price: Free trial from the Google Play Store / $2.99 to buy

Screen Adjuster

Screen Adjuster is a small, free app that allows you to set your screen's brightness below the normal minimum level. It's very useful in dark environments to avoid losing your night vision or to avoid distracting others in public venues like movie theaters. Personally, I use it before bed to minimize the impact of my Android's screen on my melatonin levels. Science!

Price: Free trial from the Google Play Store / $0.99 to buy

Shazam

Shazam uses your Android's microphone to look up the artist/name of a song. It's like Google, but for music. Depending on the audio quality and background noise, it will listen for about 5-15 seconds before telling you what you're listening to. It's very accurate and has an extensive database; very rarely does it fail to identify a song. The paid version, called Shazam Encore, removes banner advertisements.

Price: Free trial from the Google Play Store / $5.59 to buy

SMS Backup & Restore

This app allows you to backup and restore your SMS and MMS messages to your SD card or Dropbox. It works seamlessly and quickly unlike many other text message backup apps. I highly recommend using it to back up your messages or to transfer them to a new phone.

Price: Free trial from the Google Play Store / $3.49 to buy

Snes9xEX+

This app is an excellent and free Super Nintendo emulator. After you have downloaded ROM game files from the Internet, you can load them into SNES9xEX+ and play them exactly as they were on the original console. (Legal caveat: you must own the original cartridges to legally download ROM files.) Remember Super Mario World, Zelda, and Final Fantasy II/III? Great games—play them with Snes9xEx+.

The author of Snes9xEx+, Robert Broglia, sells emulators for most other classic gaming consoles as well. Snes9xEx+ is the free one that hooks you; the rest cost money, but are all excellent apps.

Price: Free from the Google Play Store

Speedtest

Speedtest is a free app that tests the speed of your Internet connection, be it Wi-Fi or cellular. It's useful to help diagnose connectivity problems, or just to show your friends how much faster your 4G LTE cell connection is than their home broadband.

Price: Free from the Google Play Store

Spotify

Spotify is a streaming music app that competes with Pandora. Unlike Pandora, however, it allows you to select one artist and listen exclusively to them for free on shuffle mode. (For the smartphone app, that is; the desktop and tablet apps actually allow you to pick any song you want at any time—even without a subscription—but with advertisements.) If you want to select songs individually on the Android smartphone app, you have to pay for the premium service. Spotify is a great complement to Pandora and has a huge library of songs (there's not much you won't find on it). If you subscribe to one streaming service, Spotify gets my vote. I have a subscription to it.

Price: Free from the Google Play Store / subscription service $9.99 per month

SuperBeam

SuperBeam is the best way to perform blazing-fast, wireless file transfers between Android devices. SuperBeam uses Wi-Fi Direct but implements it a lot more effectively than the Android OS does. When two Android phones have SuperBeam installed, they are on the same page—end of story. There's no messing around with complicated device settings like Android Beam, Wi-Fi Direct, or S Beam. I strongly recommend you use SuperBeam to transfer large files between Android devices.

Price: Free trial from the Google Play Store / $1.99 to buy

Talon for Twitter

Talon is an up-and-coming Twitter client that I like better than the official app and the other alternatives on the Google Play Store. It has great developer support, multi-account support, and costs less than $2.

Price: $1.99 from the Google Play Store

Tapatalk

If you read or participate in any online discussion forums, Tapatalk is an absolute must-have app. It condenses forum interfaces into a mobile-friendly format, and makes it much easier to read and post from your Android device. It's kind of like an RSS reader, but for forums. Tapatalk is probably one of my most-used apps—in fact, I would even use a desktop version if they made it. Nearly all major online discussion forums support Tapatalk as of 2014.

Price: Free trial from the Google Play Store / $2.99 to buy

TeamViewer

TeamViewer is a cross-platform screen-sharing program. You set up the client on your desktop computer and then access and control it from your Android phone. Yes, this means you can control your computer's screen right from your Android device! It works very well, even over slower connections. TeamViewer is incredibly cool and useful, and best of all, it's completely free for personal use.

Price: Free from the Google Play Store; desktop client available at http://www.teamviewer.com/

TeslaLED

TeslaLED is a free flashlight program that is much brighter than most built-in flashlight apps. It includes several handy widgets for quickly turning your Android's camera flash LED into a flashlight. I also really like that it doesn't request any unusual permissions at installation.

Price: Free from the Google Play Store / $1.00 optional donation

TinyShark Downloader

TinyShark Downloader lets you search for music on Grooveshark and download it to your Android device in MP3 format for playback on the music player of your choice (I suggest Google Play Music; see above). I haven't found an easier way to search for and download MP3s. Of course, be sure to only download songs to which you are legally entitled.

Price: Free from http://exigocs.com/

TouchDown For Smartphones

TouchDown is the best Microsoft Outlook replacement, bar none. It has all the built-in features of Outlook including Mail, Calendar, Tasks, and so on. If your work uses Exchange, TouchDown is simply an excellent way to keep up with your work on the go. Moreover, because it consolidates all the functions of Outlook into a single app, it creates a very nice barrier between your work life and your personal life. It's not cheap, but if you use Outlook, it's well worth it.

Price: Free trial from the Google Play Store / $19.99 to buy

TuneIn Radio

This app allows you to stream local and national AM/FM radio stations over the Internet. It's very useful for listening to radio stations in other parts of the country, for example while traveling. It can also be useful for tuning in to local stations when your regular radio reception is poor but you have a good Internet connection.

Price: Free trial from the Google Play Store / $3.99 to buy

WhatsApp Messenger

Don't have unlimited texts? No problem. Get WhatsApp and get your friends to do the same. It uses a proprietary network to send and receives text-based messages without burning through your SMS quota. There are a lot of services like WhatsApp, but it has my recommendation because it is the most popular one and your friends and family are more likely to already have it.

Price: Free from the Google Play Store

ZArchiver

ZArchiver is an archive manager compatible with a huge array of file types, including .zip, .rar, .7z, and many, many more. It is very fast, lightweight, and completely free.

Price: Free from the Google Play Store / $1.30 optional donation

BONUS: The 8 All-Time Best Root Apps

If you read Android news or discussion forums online, you are probably familiar with the term "rooting." If not, let me briefly explain.

On any Linux-based operating system, including Android, the root user is the most privileged user account on the machine and can run code that requires special administrator authorization. The root account is not normally accessible to the user. "Rooting" your Android is a procedure that allows your device to override this limitation and run code as the root user. Once rooted, you can install and use some apps that are not normally possible to use. There are thousands of root apps available, but here is a quick bonus list of my top 8:

Greenify: One flaw of Android compared to iOS is that background apps can seriously drain your battery even when you're not using them. (iOS deals with background apps in a different way that prevents this issue.) Greenify allows you to freeze these apps and reclaim battery life. If you have a lot of apps installed, you'll be amazed how much your battery life improves with Greenify.

Titanium Backup: Titanium Backup allows you to back up your apps and data to your SD card. This is useful because you can restore apps much faster from an SD card than from the Google Play Store, something that you need to do each time you install a new custom ROM while rooted. Titanium Backup has been around forever, has good developer support, and has my recommendation.

AdAway: Available from the F-Droid app repository, AdAway blocks all ads on your device. This includes ads on web pages and inside apps. It is an absolute must-have.

ROM Toolbox Pro: This app gives you several important root utilities, such as reboot to recovery and a build.prop editor. You'll eventually want or need to do these things if you root, and ROM Toolbox Pro is a great way to do them.

BetterBatteryStats: This app has unparalleled power to help you figure out the source of unknown battery drain by reporting kernel wake locks and partial wake locks. It has a steep learning curve, but once you figure out how to use it (start by Googling), you will be glad you did. Of course, if you're using Greenify, you should rarely need BetterBatteryStats.

WiFi Tether Router: In the past, many custom ROMs came with the TrevE WiFi package installed, but that app has not been updated in some time and does not work on many newer KitKat devices. WiFi Tether Router, available on the Google Play Store, allows you to tether your device's cellular connection without counting against your hotspot plan. In fact, you can even tether without paying for a hotspot plan at all. Of course, you should be aware that this might violate the terms of your contract.

Tasker: Tasker is a unique and super-powerful app. It lets you program your Android to do complex tasks in the background without your intervention. For example, you can have your Android start playing music any time it connects to your car's Bluetooth stereo, or disable the lock screen anytime you're on your home Wi-Fi network. The learning curve is even steeper than that of BetterBatteryStats, but the time investment is well worth it. To speedup the process, use Google to find Tasker tutorials.

Xposed Framework: Many root apps come in the form of Xposed plugins rather than standalone apps. You will need the Xposed Framework installed to take advantage of these plugins. I suggest installing it immediately after rooting if your custom ROM does not already include it.

Chapter 11: Accessorizing

There is a wide range of accessories available for the Note 3. In this chapter, I provide examples of both official and third party accessories, to give you an idea of what is available. I also recommend specific accessories that I have a lot of experience with. Please note that there are hundreds, if not thousands of accessories available for the Note 3 already, and it would be impossible to cover them all here. If you're interested in any of the accessories I discuss in this chapter, you should do your own research to compare prices and brands. For example, many of the official Samsung accessories I discuss have off-brand alternatives that may be just as good and/or cheaper. This chapter is only a starting point.

*TIP: If you register your Note 3 on Samsung's website (**http://www.samsung.com/us/support/register/product**), you will receive a coupon good for 50% off any mobile accessory under $50. Unfortunately, this coupon is much worse than the one offered for the Note 2 (50% off as many mobile accessories as you want, with no price limit), but it is better than nothing. After registering your Note 3, you'll receive an email entitled "Your gift for registering your Galaxy Note 3," containing your coupon code for the Samsung store.*
http://www.samsung.com/us/mobile/cell-phones-accessories

Cases

There are several types of cases for the Note 3. Personally, I use the inexpensive Cimo TPU cover (http://www.amazon.com/gp/product/B00EZD91YO), which protects the back and sides of the Note 3. TPU are soft (but firm) plastic, and their biggest advantage is that they hold their shape very well and resist stretching. I also like the Cimo case because it has textured sides that provide a much better grip on the Note 3. Similar TPU cases are available from most carriers' retail stores, although you'll likely pay 2-3 times what you would pay for a brand like Cimo online.

Sometimes, you can also find cases like the Cimo, but made of hard plastic. These are common on eBay, and usually sell directly from Asia for 3-4 dollars. However, I recommend TPU instead because of its texture and because it won't crack.

Another alternative is the Samsung S-View Flip Cover (http://www.samsung.com/us/mobile/cell-phones-accessories/EF-CN900BVESTA), which provides more functionality but less protection. It flips open and closed, and while closed, the Note 3 can display information such as the time and date through the window of the case.

If you want something heavy-duty, the OtterBox Defender is a popular solution. It provides excellent protection (including a built-in screen protector), but will substantially increase your Note 3's footprint. http://www.otterbox.com/Defender-Series-for-Samsung-Galaxy-Note-3-Case/sam2-galaxy-note-3,default,pd.html?dwvar_sam2-galaxy-note-3_color=20&start=2&cgid=samsung-galaxy-note-3-cases

Other types of cases are available but less common, such as belt holsters, pouches, kickstand cases (http://www.seidioonline.com/samsung-galaxy-note-3-surfacekickstand-combo-black-p/bd2-hr3ssgt3k-bk.htm), and even wooden cases. Amazon and eBay are good starting points to find something like this.

S Pens

Samsung sells replacement S Pens (http://www.samsung.com/us/mobile/cell-phones-accessories/ET-PN900SBESTA) that are identical to the Note 3's S Pen. It used to sell full-size S Pens with an eraser (http://www.amazon.com/Samsung-

Galaxy-S-Pen-Stylus-Eraser/dp/B009QW3SGQ). To erase, you simply flip the pen over and use the blunt top end. Samsung has discontinued this product, but it can still be found on Amazon and other sites.

Since the Note 3 uses a Wacom digitizer for S Pen input, it is also possible to use many other Wacom styli such as the Cintiq stylus. However, not all Wacom styli work equally as well and I suggest you do your own research if you're interested in purchasing a non-Samsung stylus. Personally, I find the S Pen with Eraser to be a sufficient full-size option.

Cables & Connectivity

Samsung sells a number of data and video cables for the Note 3, as well as docks.

Audio/Video

- The MHL 2.0 HDTV Smart Adapter is the simplest and cheapest way to output your Note 3's screen to an HDMI-enabled television or monitor. http://www.samsung.com/us/mobile/cell-phones-accessories/ET-H10FAUWESTA

- If you want a more full-featured solution, you can use the Smart Dock Multimedia Hub, which has HDMI, USB, and 3.5mm stereo connectors. http://www.samsung.com/us/mobile/cell-phones-accessories/EDD-S20JWEGSTA

- Alternatively, you can opt for the AllShare Cast Wireless Hub, which allows you to stream all sorts of multimedia over Wi-Fi to your HDMI television or monitor. http://www.samsung.com/us/mobile/cell-phones-accessories/EAD-T10JDEGSTA

- Finally, the Galaxy Universal Multimedia Desktop Dock is a dock designed solely to charge your Note 3 and output audio via a 3.5mm cable. It does not include HDMI or USB connectors. http://www.samsung.com/us/mobile/cell-phones-accessories/EDD-D200BEGSTA

TIP: Although the Samsung site does not yet list many of these products as compatible with the Note 3, they all are.

Data

The Note 3 uses a Micro USB 3 port. If you're like me, you had probably never seen one of these before getting your Note 3. The first thing to know about Micro

USB 3 is that it is fully compatible with Micro USB—you just need to be careful about where you jam the cable.

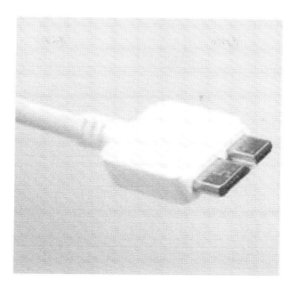

The second thing to know is that using a Micro USB 3 cable is preferable when possible, as data transfer is faster assuming the connected device also supports USB 3.0. Samsung is not yet selling Micro USB 3 cables, but you can get one at Amazon for around five dollars, if you need a replacement or an extra.

Also, consider picking up an inexpensive USB OTG cable to connect your Note 3 to flash drives, mice, keyboards, and more (http://www.amazon.com/eForCity-Adapter-compatible-Samsung%C2%A9-Galaxy/dp/B00871Q5PI). Read more about USB OTG here (p.278).

SD Cards

The Note 3 is compatible with Class 6 and 10 Micro SD memory cards, of both the SDHC and SDXC variety. Note that it does *not* support the UHS-1 standard. (You can still use UHS-1 compliant cards, but only at regular speeds.) The maximum size supported is 64 GB.

TIP: SDXC cards are no faster than SDHC cards; they simply support greater capacities. SDHC cards go up to 32 GB, so unless you need a 64 GB card, SDHC is fine.

I use SanDisk Ultra cards, which are available at very reasonable prices through Amazon.

Headsets

The Note 3 supports both wired and Bluetooth wireless headsets. (Most carriers include a basic wired headset in the box.) Samsung sells a variety of both, although Amazon has a larger selection and lower prices. Learn how to pair a Bluetooth headset here (p.235).

Batteries & Chargers

The Note 3 is a very power-hungry device, yet at the same time its battery life is among the longest of any Android phone. To accomplish this, the Note 3 uses a 3,200 mAh battery charged by a 2.0 amp charger. The Note 3's charger is much more powerful than typical smartphone chargers, and is certainly more so than any computer's USB port. For this reason, you should always charge with the provided charger or a 2.0 amp equivalent, coupled with a Micro USB 3 cable, for optimal charging times.

Samsung sells several power accessories, including standard spare batteries (http://www.samsung.com/us/mobile/cell-phones-accessories/EB-B800BUBESTA) and a spare battery charging system (http://www.samsung.com/us/mobile/cell-phones-accessories/EB-K800BUWESTA). Note that the spare battery charging system is only $10 more than a spare battery alone, and actually *includes a spare battery in the package*—so you're only paying $10 for the charger! You can also buy a wireless charging pad (http://www.samsung.com/us/mobile/cell-phones-accessories/EP-P100IJWUST2) and wireless charging cover (http://www.samsung.com/us/mobile/cell-phones-accessories/EP-CN900IBUSTA), which are compatible with the Qi wireless charging standard.

TIP: You can use a non-Samsung Qi charging pad if you wish, but make sure it is compatible with the Note 3's 2.0 amp charger for the fastest charging time.

WARNING: Although the wireless charging products are convenient, they are much slower than wired charging. Additionally, the wireless charging cover is slightly thicker than the regular cover, and may be incompatible with your case. An alternative is to buy only the wireless charging pad, and couple it with the Docooler charging receiver (http://www.amazon.com/Docooler-Standard-Wireless-Charging-Receiver/dp/B00FTULQJU/) or TechMatte charging receiver (http://www.amazon.com/gp/product/B00GMRXD9U) which fit under the normal cover and do not affect case compatibility.

Several third-party companies have also begun selling 6,400 mAh batteries, which come with thicker covers and will affect case compatibility much like Samsung's wireless charging cover. Hyperion (http://www.amazon.com/Hyperion-Extended-

Compatible-International-Warranty/dp/B00DH0JL2S/) is one option, and Anker (available on eBay) is slightly cheaper.

You can also buy rechargeable battery packs such as this one by Anker (http://www.amazon.com/Anker-Portable-Rapid-Recharge-Dual-Port-Highest-Energy-Efficiency/dp/B00DMWV3EU/), which supports 2.4 amp output. If you look at other models, make sure they support at least 2.0 amp output for the fastest charging time for your Note 3.

Also available are car chargers, and again, make sure to purchase a unit with a high enough current output such as this one (http://www.amazon.com/Release-Anker%C2%AE-2-4A-4-8A-Charger/dp/B00EE4A9SQ/).

Screen Protectors

There are countless brands of screen protectors, some of which are only a couple dollars or less per pack. However, I suggest purchasing quality screen protectors for the Note 3, to ensure optimal clarity and S Pen functionality.

I have been a long time user of Spigen screen protectors, and recommend them wholeheartedly. The cheaper PET film version is quite good (http://www.amazon.com/Samsung-Protector-Crystal-JAPANESE-Premium/dp/B00DD5TUZ0/), and is a much better value than the more expensive tempered glass version.

If you want something other than Spigen, iSmooth is decent. The iloome ScreenMate screen protector (http://www.amazon.com/iloome-ScreenMate-Flexible-Protector-Oleophobic/dp/B00G5POLCM/) has also received very favorable reviews. If you are indifferent, my suggestion is Spigen because I know and trust the brand.

Vehicle Docks

Samsung sells a Universal Vehicle Navigation Mount (http://www.samsung.com/us/mobile/cell-phones-accessories/ECS-K200BEGSTA) for the Galaxy series, which is compatible with the Note 3. It is useful both for improving hands-free access, as well as if you plan to use your Note 3 as your main GPS. Another popular and cheaper option is the iOttie dashboard mount (http://www.amazon.com/iOttie-Windshield-Dashboard-Holder-Galaxy/dp/B007FH716W/).

Other

Other accessories for the Note 3 include, but are not limited to:

- **NFC TecTiles** (read more (p.273)): These are programmable RFID stickers. You can place them around your home, car, and office, and execute custom actions when you tap your Note 3 against them. The Note 3 is compatible with both original TecTiles (http://www.amazon.com/Samsung-TecTiles-Programmable-Communication-Enabled/dp/B0089VO7RY) and TecTiles 2 (http://www.amazon.com/TecTiles-5-Pack-Programmable-Communication-Samsung/dp/B00DKXXLNC/). They do exactly the same thing, but TecTiles 2 uses a more future-proof standard and is a better choice if you think you might want to use your TecTiles with future phones.

- **The Galaxy Gear Smartwatch**: The Galaxy Gear was released alongside the Note 3 and works as a companion device via Bluetooth, showing notifications and allowing control over features such as media and calls. However, the Galaxy Gear was reviewed poorly and many believe that users would be better served by waiting for the next model.

- **Various Other Peripherals**: Bluetooth keyboards, etc.

Mailing List

To thank you for purchasing *Samsung Galaxy Note 3: The 100% Unofficial User Guide*, I would like to offer you a chance to receive FREE Note 3 news, tips & tricks, app recommendations, and more in your email inbox. Please take a minute to sign up:

http://www.aaronhalbert.com/phplist/?p=subscribe&id=1

February 2014 Update: Android 4.4.2 Kit Kat

WHAT: The Note 3 originally shipped with the Android 4.3 Jelly Bean operating system, but as of February 2014 the Kit Kat 4.4.2 update is imminent. Kit Kat will bring some new features to your Note 3, so read on to get the full scoop.

WHEN: You can expect the official Kit Kat over-the-air update sometime in February or March 2014. None of the major U.S. carriers have announced a firm date, but most industry watchers agree it won't be much longer. It is possible, though unlikely, that Kit Kat will be delayed past March.

HOW: When the update is released, your Note 3 will display a notification screen with installation instructions. If you accidentally dismiss it, just restart your Note 3 and it will appear again.

***

In this bonus chapter, I will explain Kit Kat's new features one-by-one. I'd say the Kit Kat update is a 'grab bag'—lots of new, small additions, but no major changes that will require you to relearn your Note 3. Overall, I give it a thumbs-up. Enjoy the preview!

***

- **Safety Assistance Feature**: There is now an emergency alert you can activate by holding Volume Up and Volume Down together for three seconds. This will take pictures using your front and back cameras and send them, along with your GPS location, to your choice of emergency contacts. Keep in mind that this feature will only work if you have an Internet connection. I suggest testing it in advance if you decide to enable it.

  To enable Safety Assistance and specify your emergency contacts, go to Device Settings → General → Safety Assistance.

- **Google Cloud Print**: This feature was available in 4.3 Jelly Bean, but required a separate download from the Play Store. It's now baked directly into the operating system, so you can wirelessly print files from your Note 3 with ease. To get started, you'll need to visit https://www.google.com/cloudprint/ and set up your printer with Google Cloud Print. After that's done, you'll be able to print from Android apps such as Quickoffice (free from the Play Store), Chrome, and more. To do so, look for a "Print" option, or a "Share" option and choose to share via Google Cloud Print.

- **Media Controls on Lock Screen**: On 4.3 Jelly Bean, if your Note 3 went to sleep while playing music or streaming video through HDMI or a Chromecast, you would have to wake it and clear the lock screen to pause or change tracks. Kit Kat makes this process easier by including media controls on the lock screen itself. So, if you have a PIN lock, for example, you'll no longer need to enter it to switch songs or pause your movie.

- **Full-Screen Art on Lock Screen**: In addition to media controls, the lock screen also now features full-screen artwork when you're listening to an album or streaming a movie to another device. If you don't see this, it's probably because the file you're playing doesn't have any artwork encoded in it. In such a case, you'll see placeholder artwork instead (a music note or a movie reel). This feature works with the stock Music app, as well as some third-party apps such as Spotify.

- **Emojis Built in to the Samsung Keyboard**: Emojis have been popular on Japanese phones for quite some time, and are making their way to the rest of the world. They are smiley-like icons primarily intended for use in text messages, much like emoticons. Of course, many phones already convert text-based emoticons like :-) to pictures, but Emojis are a little different. First, Emojis come only in picture form, and second, there is a huge variety to choose from. There are dog Emojis, building Emojis, policeman Emojis, and more.

To try Emojis, bring up the Samsung keyboard, tap "Sym," and then the smiley face icon. One caveat is that if you send Emojis to friends with non-Android phones, they may see garbled characters or nothing at all. Another caveat is that if you send a text message with an Emoji from the Messages app, the Note 3 will send the message as an MMS, which may result in extra charges depending on your data plan. Most phones can send Emojis through regular SMS messages, so hopefully Samsung will fix this feature soon. (Alternatively, you can send SMS messages from the Hangouts app, which has proper support for Emojis.)

- **Launcher and SMS App Switching Menu**: There is now a dedicated settings menu for choosing your default launcher and text-messaging app. To access it, go to Device Settings → General → Default Applications. This is useful if you have installed a third-party launcher like Nova Launcher but want to return to the stock launcher, or if you want to always use Hangouts to send and receive text messages instead of Samsung's Messages app. In 4.3 Jelly Bean, it was much more complicated to change these settings, so this is a nice addition.

- **Galaxy Gear Improvements**: If you use your Note 3 with a Samsung Galaxy Gear smart watch, you will notice better connectivity and improved email notification options with Kit Kat. Make sure your Galaxy Gear software is updated in the Play Store to take full advantage of these improvements.

- **Improved Landscape Keyboard**: Samsung has compressed the layout of the landscape keyboard, making it more thumb-friendly.

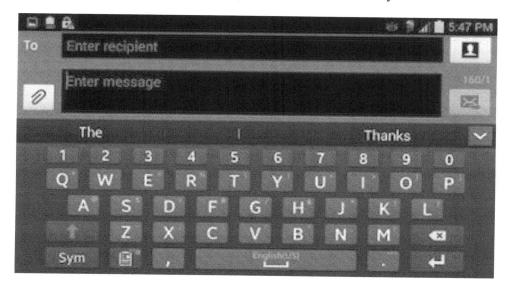

- **Improved Cloud Storage Integration**: Kit Kat gives apps better ways of interfacing with cloud storage services such as Google Drive and Dropbox. For example, Quickoffice (free from the Play Store) now allows you to open and edit files directly from your cloud drive without first copying them to your Note 3. I particularly like this feature, because editing a file on your cloud drive means the changes are instantly backed up. This was not the case in the past, when you had to copy files to your Note 3 before editing them. Be aware that it may take time for app developers to update their apps to include this feature.

- **Lower Power Audio Playback**: Kit Kat consumes less battery power than Jelly Bean while playing audio, so you can listen to MP3s or Pandora for longer than ever before.

- **Aesthetic Changes**: Google has made a few changes to Kit Kat's graphic interface. For example, you will notice that your home screen wallpaper now extends from the very top to the very bottom of your screen. You'll also notice that all icons in the status bar are now solid white. In my opinion, this particular change is a step backward. Android 4.3 Jelly Bean identified your connectivity status using colored icons, which no longer exist in Kit Kat.

- **Immersive App Mode**: In Immersive Mode, an app can hide the status bar to achieve a full-screen effect, but importantly, allow you to recall the status bar by swiping down from the top of the screen. In the past, full screen apps existed, but there was no way to access the status bar without exiting the apps. I expect Immersive Mode to become a popular feature of apps like Amazon Kindle and video players. Note that Immersive Mode must be enabled by an app's developer at the time of programming; it's not a feature you can enable on your own.

- **Bluetooth MAP Support**: Bluetooth MAP promises improvements to phone-car integration, and is becoming more popular in newer model year cars. Kit Kat now offers full support for this protocol.

- **Chrome Web View**: In the past, it was possible for apps to display web pages, but that was accomplished using the default Internet browser engine. In Kit Kat, developers can render web content in their apps using the Chrome engine. In practical terms, this means that web pages displayed inside apps will be faster.

- **Support for Tap-and-Pay Payments (Maybe)**: The Note 3, and many other popular Android phones, contain an NFC chip compatible with tap-and-pay technology. So in theory, tap-and-pay should already be widely available on Android phones. Unfortunately, the process has been bogged down by carrier politics and technical problems.

Kit Kat fixes the technical issues once and for all, but there are rumors that the carriers have gone to extra lengths to disable this new fix. (!) So, it is possible, but uncertain whether tap-and-pay will work when the official Kit Kat update comes to the Note 3. Once you get Kit Kat, you can attempt to configure tap-and-pay by downloading Google Wallet from the Play Store, but if you have errors setting it up, you'll know why.

- **Email App Redesigned**: The default Email app has always lagged behind the Gmail app in terms of looks and functionality. With Kit Kat, Google has totally revamped Email to bring it up to par. Email is your go-to app if you need to set up a non-Gmail account like Yahoo.

- **Closed-Captioning Support**: You can enable Closed Captioning by going to Device Settings → Device → Accessibility. (Turn on both Google and Samsung Closed Captioning.) Any apps that have subtitled videos will now show captions as the video plays. Note that this will not magically enable Closed Captioning for all videos you watch on your Note 3; it only works if an app developer has taken the time to program in the transcript for the video in his or her app. So, don't expect this to provide captioning for YouTube videos or movies you copy to your SD card.

- **Faster Screen Unlock**: Unlocking your screen is much faster in Kit Kat than in Jelly Bean. You'll notice that your Note 3 processes your swipe, PIN code, pattern, or other unlocking action much faster than it did before.

- **Camera Shortcut on Lock Screen**: The Kit Kat lock screen now has a small camera icon in the bottom-right-hand corner. You can swipe this up and to the left to quickly open the Camera app from your lock screen, giving you a better chance to capture fleeting moments. It is also possible to change this icon to open an app other than Camera, if you want. To do so, go to Device Settings → Device → Lock Screen → Shortcuts.

- **Performance Upgrades**: In addition to all the new features mentioned above, Kit Kat also includes numerous behind-the-scenes performance optimizations. In practical terms, you can expect fewer app crashes and faster overall performance. With 3 GB of RAM and a 2.3 GHz quad-core processor, the Note 3 was already doing fine—but every bit helps.

- **Easter Egg**: An Easter Egg is a fun, hidden feature that an app developer programs into his or her software as a sort of calling card. Kit Kat has a tasty-looking one. Go to Device Settings → General → About Device and keep tapping on "Android Version." You will see a big "K" appear. Keep tapping to see some animations and a Kit Kat-inspired Android logo.

There are also a few Kit Kat features that Samsung has chosen not to include in the Note 3 update:

- **The Google Experience Launcher**: OEM Kit Kat devices such as the Nexus series feature the Google Experience Launcher, a launcher that allows you to bring up Google Now by saying "OK, Google" any time your device is on the home screen or app drawer. Since all of Samsung's devices use its proprietary TouchWiz launcher, this Kit Kat feature won't be coming to the Note 3. However, you can still get the Google Experience Launcher on your Note 3 if you're willing to do some legwork. For more information, see this web page: http://www.droid-life.com/2014/02/05/the-google-now-launcher-is-coming-it-will-even-import-from-your-old-launcher/

- **Pseudo-Caller ID**: The stock Kit Kat phone app includes a new feature that searches Google to identify incoming calls—a poor man's caller ID. Again, because Samsung uses its own dialer app, you won't find this feature on the Note 3.

- **Magazine UX**: If you've read about the upcoming Tab Pro and Note Pro tablets, you might be familiar with the next-generation Samsung user interface called Magazine UX. This didn't make it in the Note 3 Kit Kat upgrade. Rumors suggest that the upcoming Galaxy S5 will be the first Samsung phone to feature the new Magazine UX.

- **Android Run Time (ART)**: ART is a new feature of Kit Kat that helps devices run faster and use less battery while sleeping. Unfortunately, it's been left out of the Note 3 Kit Kat update.

There's also one downright ugly change: If you have a third-party S-View case for the Note 3, like the Spigen Slim Armor View, your case will no longer function. Samsung has blocked third-party cases in favor of its own S-View case. This was an unfortunate decision by Samsung, and shows a lack of respect for its customers. Unless they decide to reverse course, the only way to defeat this new limitation is to root your Note 3 and install Xposed Framework, a fairly complicated process. See more information here: http://forum.xda-developers.com/showthread.php?p=49664676

As I mentioned at the beginning of this chapter, the major U.S. carriers are expected to release the Kit Kat update in February or March. It is possible, but unlikely, that Kit Kat will arrive for the Note 3 later than March. When it is available for your device, you will automatically receive a notification and instructions to complete the upgrade.

I hope you've enjoyed this Kit Kat preview. If you have any questions, feel free to shoot me an email at AJH@AaronHalbert.com.

-Aaron Halbert

2/16/2014

33887684R00184

Made in the USA
Lexington, KY
14 July 2014